Concept and Composition

the basis of successful art

Concept and Composition

Fritz Henning

North Light Publishers

*Two and two make four. But a
picture to be worth remembering
must add up to more than the
sum of its parts.*

Albin Henning (1886-1943)

Published by NORTH LIGHT PUBLISHERS, an imprint of
WRITER'S DIGEST BOOKS, 9933 Alliance Road,
Cincinnati, Ohio 45242

Library of Congress Cataloging in Publication Data
Henning, Fritz, 1920-
     Concept and composition.
     Bibliography: p.
     Includes index.
     1. Painting—Technique. 2. Perception.
3. Composition (Art) I. Title.
ND1475.H45 1983   750'.1   83-2319
ISBN 0-89134-059-9
ISBN 0-89134-060-2 (pbk.)

Albin Henning, *rough compositional sketch*

Dedication

This book is written for the younger generation;
in particular, four fine representatives of it—
my children:
    Rick—the achiever
    Mark—the idealist
    Ann—the mother and organizer
    Jo—the singer of songs

Acknowledgments

An author's job is always a lonely one, but the task is ineluctably lightened by a variety of helpers. Of special note in producing this work is my debt to all the artists, present and past, whose pictures give meaning and purpose to the text. Thanks are due to Carla Dennis, whose thoughtful editorial advice and literal interpretation of the written word aided immensely in overcoming areas of confusion. Sincere bows go to Ben Stahl for encouragement and for the generous use of so much of his work. My old colleague Walt Reed was most helpful, opening the doors of his unsurpassed collection of illustrations. Also, I am indebted to Charles B. Ferguson and his able staff at the New Britain Museum of American Art, as well as many other museums throughout the world, for their cooperation. Most of all, I am grateful to my wife Jane for her patience in putting up with my extended tours of isolation in my backlot studio. And to Chester for his loyal support in that isolation.

Ben Stahl

Contents

← Nicolai Fechin

Rembrandt
Self-Portrait, Etching

Enlarged reproduction.
Original etching is but two inches high.

Preface

The title of this book, *Concept and Composition*, describes its contents as inclusively and succinctly as possible. It's a short title, and clearly suggests what this offering is all about. That these two considerations are essential to successful art is undeniable. At the same time, the scope and purpose of the book may be somewhat clouded because *concept* used as an art term is often misunderstood. And this lack of comprehension is not limited to the nonartist and the neophyte. Many skilled professionals have difficulty in this area. For these reasons, a few prefatory remarks seem in order to properly set the stage for the serious reader.

This is not a *how-to* art book. In fact it deals with *pre*-how-to—the first, most important steps in creating a picture. It is a teaching assemblage concentrating on the prerequisite conditions and thinking all artists, and would-be artists, should practice if their skills and techniques are to produce rewarding results. It covers areas many skip in the study of art, and their work often suffers because of it.

Concept and *composition* are customarily glossed over in all manner of art education, whether book or classroom. Concept, in particular, is ignored as a misty substance too intangible to understand, while composition is usually limited to stereotyped, formularized solutions. Here, through examples, and as much as possible with the words of an assortment of knowledgeable artists, these elusive, ignored specters are dragged from the dark closet and examined.

The text and illustrations are directed to everyone interested in art—but especially to all artists, both experienced and novice. In many ways, and in many cases, the gulf separating the trained from the untutored in this area is not as great as you might imagine.

Too many artists who consider themselves experienced practitioners do so on the basis of technical proficiency and craftsmanship. Sadly, a large percentage of them are noticeably (to all, it seems, but themselves) deficient in understanding the importance of picture concept. In addition, they often rely on dogma and a comfortable tried-and-sure system to solve their compositional problems. They are, without realizing it, mired on a dead-end street of catchall visual clichés. It is likely they could advance in their artistic attainment if they took serious stock of their initial approach to picture ideas. It is hoped the examples anthologized on these pages will kindle the spark of awareness, making it possible for some of these capable individuals to achieve fuller creative maturity.

Thoughts for beginners

Experience shows many people who would like to take a fling at painting are put off by misconceptions about their artistic ability. Artists, they feel, must be born under the right star and endowed with gifts beyond the norm. Some are, of course, but if you limit your vision to Michelangelo, Leonardo, Rembrandt, Degas and the like, you will be denying the considerable accomplishments of the multitude of artists who have gained personal satisfaction and, at times, even fame and fortune by starting at a level far below the exceptional category. A half-millennium ago the great German artist Albrecht Dürer had this to say on the subject: "Some are able to learn all manner of arts, but not all have that capacity. But, no man of sense is so rude he is not able to learn something to which his spirit most inclines him." Doubt not that individual "spirit," propelled by sustaining interest, has been the impetus for many creditable artistic accomplishments.

Understandably, the novice's hobgoblin of self-doubt may be fueled when initial efforts fall short of expectations. Working alone—and the creative process is always a lonely one—everyone encounters early and continued disappointments. Why should creating pictures be considered in a different light than mastering other disciplines? Did Pavarotti never falter in his quest for voice control? Did Baryshnikov never stumble in a leap? Not likely. With few exceptions, quick success is not the rule in worthwhile endeavors.

On the other hand, if your interest in art is a casual, sometimes thing, you might as well forget it. The way of art is tough for the faint-hearted. But don't toss in the towel if you have the desire, yet feel you lack talent. There is ample evidence nearly everyone has a reservoir of ability. If you have a genuine interest, stick with it and make the most of what you have. More artistic accomplishments come about through interest combined with effort than by talent not on speaking terms with toil.

Creativity and picture ideas

Another area of confusion is *talent's* kissing cousin, *creativity*. We all know this is hallowed ground. For certain, there is little of substance to stand on in this mushy bog, and the tract is clearly posted by a tremulous teaching profession as a field of quicksand to be avoided. Creativity, we are told, cannot be taught. That the task is difficult will not be denied, but the totality of truth in the assumption is open to challenge. Based on considerable experience in observing, studying, teaching, and practicing the enigmatic ways of picture making, it is apparent to me artists are quite capable of learning much about the creative process, even if specific procedures are not easily systematized.

So, if you have the "spirit" Dürer describes and are ready to work at the job, be assured you can harness sufficient creativity and talent to produce rewarding pictures. Read on.

To be worth anything pictures must be based on an idea that grows out of the individual's psyche and personal experience. Every visualization is molded in accordance with our background, our culture, and our reaction to the source of motivation. Few ideas of substance come to us full-blown and ready to be executed in final form. Even after a visual idea gains shape it is unlikely to remain unscathed in the process of being forged into a picture. The whole procedure grows something like a game of solitaire—the black 7 goes on a red 8, which in turn triggers another shift, and so on. With pictures, the maze of interrelated elements—subjects, shape, line, tone, pattern, texture, color—offers a range of possible solutions as confusing as Rubik's cube. With every stroke of the pencil or brush the artist is confronted with new avenues of pictorial possibilities. Even the experienced professional is seldom able to forecast that which is yet to unfold.

It is in this caldron of constant search, and moment-to-moment decision making that the stuff of artistic creativity is molded. There is not so much mystery about it as there is dogged work. Each interim step is formulated by intuition supported by trial and error. Practice and experience will make things easier, but never, ever, is it a sure thing.

Creativity in any form is something short of an exact science. The path up the yellow brick road is as erratic as the course of an elliptical billiard ball. No one can say "Do this, that, and the next" and expect anything but a conventional, formularized product as a result. Conversely, if you approach your picture on the basis the idea and design are evolutionary, give yourself time, and are willing to put in the effort, you will surely generate some sparks that can be properly called *creative*.

This contention is supported in practice by a great range of artists, following diverse approaches, as this book will demonstrate. No less an authority than the indefatigable wizard of watercolor, Edgar A. Whitney, in his ninetieth year penned: "Competence can be acquired and taste educated."

Now that we have cleared away whatever intimidating doubts you might harbor as to anyone's potential in the talent and creative departments, let's get on with it and confront two profoundly fascinating aspects of art. What do you have to lose? Nothing, perhaps, but some misconceptions.

Fritz Henning
Weston, Connecticut, 1982

Introduction

Most of us take for granted the approach universally used in the teaching and learning process. No matter how simple or complex the discipline we strive to make our own, we attack in the same manner. One way or another, every subject is sliced into chewable bits. From algebra to zoology, we seek proficiency the same way we climb a steep stairway. At first our enthusiasm allows us to bound ahead, taking two or more risers at a stride; but soon, a little out of breath, we content ourselves with the more manageable pace of one small step at a time.

So it is with the study of art. What could be more logical when undertaking the bewildering intricacies of picture making than chipping away at the outer edges of an unfathomable core? Divide and conquer. If we can digest the small pieces we should be able to master the whole. And that is the way to go about it. Possibly it is the only way. The snag inevitably comes when the several pieces fail to fit together like the preordained finale of a jigsaw puzzle. Some key ingredient always seems to be missing or in short supply.

The means of creating pictures can be readily identified. With the possible exception of some avant-garde devotees who operate without benefit of standards, an artist, to be worthy of the name in our culture, must be cognizant of the cornerstones of Western art: drawing, design, and the ways of light and color. He should also bring to each project a multitude of technical facilities; and it is helpful to have in his kit a few rendering tricks to sprinkle the aggregate with a touch of magic. Given these ingredients, and many lay claim to them, we might expect a steady stream of pictures worthy of viewing and serious contemplation. Not often does this happen. Why? The reason is as simple as the remedy is elusive.

A disquieting number of experienced artists, as well as most beginners, fail to recognize it takes more than skillful drawing, dazzling technique, control of color, and tricks to a worthy picture make. True, these elements are important, but without a provocative *concept* soundly *composed*, the results will be as rewarding as a losing lottery ticket. Sadly, much fine work is wasted for want of sufficient preliminary thought and planning. The craftsman is so eager to display his skills that he builds his picture structure on a shallow base.

Concept and *composition* are the bedrock on which a picture succeeds or fails. Composition can be isolated in much the same manner as perspective, form, anatomy and the like are studied. Such segregated analysis is useful, and much of the latter part of this book is directed toward that end. As important as composition is in its own right, the serious reader is enjoined to constantly consider composition as the servant of the picture concept. Concept should always shine through a composition like a shaft of sunlight piercing gray clouds. A picture unclear in concept and lacking the support of a functional composition, is about as effective as a song without a melody, or a story without conflict.

What, then, is this pervasive, pivotal element—picture concept?* How can it be collared and brought to heel?

If you haven't already guessed, you will soon discover there are no easy, simplistic answers to these questions. There are no absolutes on which to hang your paint-encrusted smock. You'll never be able to say: "This is it, you rascal, I know the secret; evermore I can control my picture concept as deftly as I maneuver my favorite brush." Never!

Picture concept is the *idea* that takes visual form. It germi-

Jan Vermeer
Kunsthistorisches Museum, Vienna

nates through the mechanism called the creative process, sometimes inspiration. It matters not what you call it so long as its primacy is recognized. It is the thought process formulated by the artist enabling him to make a visual statement in response to some inner or outward motivation. It can be initiated by a scene, event, memory, the atmosphere, or any subconscious mental image or mood. As in all things creative, there are no predictable formulas. Each individual and circumstance is different. Inspiration blooms from varied and unpredictable stimuli.

The examples and analyses offered here should coax you to a broader understanding of the mercurial elements essential to the creation of meaningful pictures. Whether you are a practicing artist, a beginner, or an individual curious about the ways of art, your application and appreciation should start with knowledge of concept and composition. This is the beginning of it all: the capital A of Art. All else is secondary.

*Picture concept as discussed throughout this book has no relationship to concept art as defined by Marcel Duchamp in 1913. Duchamp's theory was to de-emphasize art in the traditional sense. He saw the role of the artist as one of selecting "ready-made" things for aesthetic consideration rather than that of manipulating paint and other materials. The act of selection of itself he purported to be the artistic accomplishment. Largely under this banner the Dada and later "anti-art" movements developed. Primarily, artists of this bent decry all tradition and standards. They feel free to suggest anything as a work of art. Since they have no desire to communicate directly with the observer, the viewer is left to see in the offering whatever he wishes. There appears little of lasting merit in such an approach. It serves mainly as a spoof aimed at a bewildered public.

← **Robert Fawcett**
Sketches of a left-handed student

Rembrandt
National Gallery, London

Concept

The thing that hath been, it is that which shall be; and that which is done is that which shall be done: and there is no new thing under the sun.

Ecclesiastes 1:9

PROFESSOR BUTTS GETS HIS WHISKERS CAUGHT IN A LAUNDRY WRINGER AND AS HE COMES OUT THE OTHER END HE THINKS OF AN IDEA FOR A SIMPLE PARACHUTE. AS AVIATOR JUMPS FROM PLANE FORCE OF WIND OPENS UMBRELLA (A) WHICH PULLS CORD (B) AND CLOSES SHEARS (C), CUTTING OFF CORNER OF FEATHER PILLOW (D). AS WHITE FEATHERS (E) FLY FROM PILLOW, PENGUIN (F) MISTAKES THEM FOR SNOW FLAKES AND FLAPS HIS WINGS FOR JOY WHICH DRAWS BUCK-SAW (G) BACK AND FORTH CUTTING LOG OF WOOD (H). AS PIECE OF WOOD FALLS INTO BASKET (I) ITS WEIGHT CAUSES ROPE (J) TO PULL TRIGGER OF GUN (K) WHICH EXPLODES AND SHOOTS LOCK FROM CAGE (L) RELEASING GIANT UMPHA BIRD (M) WHICH FLIES AND KEEPS AVIATOR AFLOAT WITH ROPE (N). AVIATOR BREAKS PAPER BAG OF CORN (O) CAUSING CORN TO FALL TO GROUND. WHEN BIRD SWOOPS DOWN TO EAT CORN, FLIER UNHOOKS APPARATUS AND WALKS HOME.
THE BIGGEST PROBLEM IS WHERE TO GET THE UMPHA BIRD. WRITE YOUR CONGRESSMAN.

The search for ideas

Some years ago I had the good fortune of being involved in a meeting organized to explore the less-than-esoteric topic: *problem solving in business*. It proved to be a memorable experience, not because it led to solutions of business problems (it didn't), but because it revealed some provocative insights about the way ideas are generated. Since every picture starts with an idea, it follows that, all else being equal, the better the idea the better the result. It seems prudent, then, to investigate all we can about the modus operandi of brewing brainstorms.

Despite some enduring myths, such as Isaac Newton discovering the law of gravity as the result of being zonked by a falling apple, good ideas seldom appear in lightning flashes. Most often they develop through a protracted incubation period, finding the light of day only after tedious pecking at a translucent shell of murky generalities. This fact was reinforced in startling ways at the aforementioned meeting.

One of the speakers was a member of a consulting company who specialized in finding solutions to other people's insoluble problems. Their product was creative thinking—a think tank for hire. They had many and varied clients, and they were successful. This is the way the operation worked.

After a problem was identified, several individuals of diverse backgrounds and training were assembled. The group,

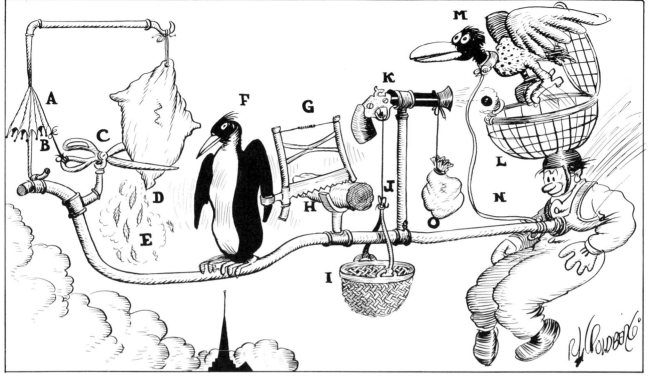

usually made up of four or five people, representing an assortment of disciplines, included a scientist, a historian or other scholar, an engineer, and a member of the arts, most often an artist or writer. The composition of the task force depended on the subject at hand. Whatever the case, the ground rules were the same. Here is an example of a solution to one of the problems presented.

The client was the U.S. Department of Defense. Understandably, the Army wanted to effectively conceal from high-flying observers, all vehicles and tanks traveling through open, unscreened areas. Standard camouflage painting techniques were not sufficiently effective. Problem: Find a means of disguising such vehicles. The remedy must be light in weight, easy to handle and operable within ten seconds.

After the problem was explained in detail a deep silence enveloped the assembled thinkers. The quiet was soon broken when one of the men left his chair at the conference table and began flapping his arms as if he were a bird trying to take off. He then made some cooing sounds and fell to the floor with his arms outstretched. When his colleagues asked what he was doing he said he was trying to act out the antics he had observed a quail go through after sighting a hawk overhead.

"Ah," said another member, "what would the bird accomplish by spreading its wings? Knowingly or not, he would be attempting to diffuse the shadow of his shape, and by so doing make himself less visible."

From this simple thought the salient issue became apparent to all. No matter how well the vehicles were camouflaged with color and design, their shadows in open areas would be unmistakably visible from above. The answer then must include finding a way to eradicate the vehicle's shadow. Covering the machines with a tarpaulin was suggested, but no one was able to figure how such an operation could be accomplished within a few seconds, or how the tarp could be spread to eliminate the telltale shadow. Then someone thought there might be a way of using balloons to do the job. A possibility, but in a wink the mention of balloons triggered in another member the image of children's birthday parties. What are those paper things kids blow on and they unroll in your face? Almost immediately they all knew they were onto something.

In short order sketches were made showing how a lightweight series of plastic tubes, coiled in a neat package atop the vehicle would do the job. One turn of a valve on a connecting compressed air tank would instantaneously inflate camouflaged spider-like tentacles that would extend outward in all directions forming an irregular pattern, effectively obliterating the giveaway shadows. The rig was easy to use, light, fast-operating, inexpensive, and it worked.

If you think this sounds as bizarre as a Rube Goldberg scenario in quest of an Umpha bird, you are not far off. The speaker's additional examples of merry-go-round think tank approaches confirmed the fact that a journey to idea-land is likely to follow weird and wonderful courses.

As extraordinary as such idea sleuthing may seem, we are forced to admit its efficacy. Good ideas are elusive. They will seldom expose themselves on direct push-button command. Nor do they seem susceptible to a frontal attack. At best, an idea can be lured from hiding in roundabout, devious, step-by-step fashion.

With the support of ancient wisdom and tons of historical and scientific precedent, we can be sure there is, indeed, nothing new under the sun. What we need is a divining rod to tell us where to dig. The think tanks have their kind of forked stick to help them find their way. Individuals usually can't operate in quite the same manner, but we all have resources we seldom tap. When we learn to stretch our capacities and search, we are on our way to becoming artists with ideas.

Albrecht Dürer

Artists interpreting artists at work . . .

Throughout the ages artists have recorded their studio environment in a great variety of ways. Many have tried their hand at self-portraits, and given posterity fascinating insights into their personalities. Here and on the following pages are a number of examples of how artists saw themselves and their studios.

Unknown Flemish artist, fifteenth century
New York Public Library

Katherina van Hemessen
Offentliche Kunstsammlung, Basel, Switzerland

Rembrandt *Museum of Fine Arts, Boston, Zoe Oliver Sherman Collection*

After-the-fact solutions to most problems look simple and hardly worth all the fuss. Would they were so obvious at the outset when the mind was as blank as the pristine paper. It is a hard fact of life that good solutions, even to elemental problems, are seldom achieved without search and effort. Never is this more true than when considering picture concepts. There are always so many ways to express every subject. The variety of pictures illustrating this section, all dealing with the same theme—the artist at work—supplies a small sampling of the scope of approaches open for even the most limited subjects.

How is the neophyte to know which approach is best? Again, there are no simple answers. The way you determine

Joshua Reynolds, *Self-Portrait*

your picture concept must be based on *your* reaction to the subject. Your solution will be governed by your life experience as it is reflected in your quest for your personal means of expression. The important thing is to give your search a chance. Don't settle for the quick, easy, and obvious. You have more to offer than a superficial stereotyped approach. Don't pretend you can compensate for a hackneyed concept with superlative rendering and sparkling techniques. Such niceties may confuse the uninformed, but they won't work for the long haul.

Most artists soon discover that if the basic idea of their picture is good, the concept clearly expressed, viewers will appreciate the statement even if they find a fault or deficiency in some aspect of the work. The reverse of this is seldom true. The original idea translated into a sound picture concept overrides all other considerations in the development of a meaningful work of art.

Multiple stimuli

Every picture has its inception in some kind of an idea. We see, feel, react to an inner urge, and attempt to crystallize our responses in some visual form. For most of us the first picture concept we come up with is likely to be in a realistic—probably a photographic—framework. This is understandable and to be expected. We are all products of our culture, and our environment from earliest memory is imbued with images having their origin in some type of photography. But how we

Honoré Daumier
Museum of Art, Rheims

actually observe is considerably different than the facsimile stemming from the mechanisms of a cyclopic box. In particular, the still camera, that indispensable crutch of many artists, is a poor substitute for our own vision and personal reaction to the subject.

Anyone blessed with reasonable eyesight enjoys many advantages over the camera. We have two eyes and can discern depth far better than the camera; our vision is more adaptable to the scene before us and is not restricted to a split-second of time. As to color, there are definite limitations between what we actually view and the chemical approximation of the scene as recorded on film or tape. Our other senses also have a profound bearing on our responses. We can hear the birds and thunder, feel the wind and rain, touch rocks and know their texture, and smell the ripe grain and blossoms and know their kind.

These sensations are only a part of the stimuli we constantly encounter. Not to try to express them in our visual statement is to shortchange ourselves and our audience. Settling for the obvious, conventional picture concept is like putting to sea in the fog without a compass. It may be possible to stumble onto a safe course and ultimately arrive at the destination, but chances are against it. The journey will more likely end in disaster.

Seeing and perceiving

We all put much stock in our perception of things. Seeing is believing, and we know what we *see* is gospel. Some modern scholars believe "Vision is the primary medium of thought,"* while the Roman encyclopedist—Pliny, two thousand years ago turned the statement around when he said, "The mind is the real instrument of sight and observation." The nineteenth-century New Englander Henry David Thoreau gave it another twist when he argued, "The eye sees for the hand but not for the mind." Whatever your predilection in this arena may be, you will probably agree with W.K. Lockard, who wrote, "Vision is our best-developed sense, and the unique linkage of remarkable vision with a facile hand is the source of [our] intelligence."**

As profound as all this may sound, the fact remains we all see things differently. This is true because our reactions to what we see are based on our mental conditioning to the subject. All of us are limited by our point of view, our knowledge, and our particular bias. This is as it should be because what we express should reflect our attitude. Not to do so would skirt the truth as we understand it and inevitably, no matter how well intended, diminish the force of our statement. Most artists come to know that compromise in a picture is a reef in the sail of effectiveness.

Along with the individuality of our visual responses we should be aware the audience viewing our work carries with them their own pack of prejudices. Artists should take cognizance of this fact, but they should not be dissuaded by it. What we intend and expect our picture to express may be interpreted quite differently by the viewer. Even so, the artist has no reason to offer explanations outside the dimensions of the picture itself. You must go it alone, and your picture should stand on its own. In the long run it is far wiser to paint to please yourself than to try to second-guess what others *may* like. (Such an approach, of course, is not always possible when working as an illustrator or commerical artist—a major reason much capable work produced in these fields falls short when viewed as art.)

It is unlikely there is a person in the world who does not believe he *sees* things "naturally" and just as they really are. Yet,

Rosa Bonheur
Uffizi, Florence

*From *Visual Thinking* by Rudolf Arnheim
**From *Design Drawing* by William Kirby Lockard

Georges Seurat

Philadelphia Museum of Art

Vincent van Gogh

Stedelijk Museum, Amsterdam

as inborn as the act of seeing is to us, there are many things we must *learn* to see. Did you ever look through a microscope, a telescope, or a pair of binoculars? What you see through these magnifiers is "natural" also, but such expanded perspective establishes quite a different visual environment. Such *seeing* must be learned. Much of what we take for granted as part of our normal vision is in fact an acquired ability largely influenced by our cultural heritage. Here are a couple of examples to explain this sometimes obscure point.

In the early years of World War II many American flyers in the South Pacific, Africa, and some other areas, carried special identification papers as part of their bail-out gear. The purpose was to help explain the airman's presence if he were forced down in lands occupied by primitive people. Because of the great variety of tribal languages, most without written form, the military believed the best way to communicate with the natives would be through the medium of pictures. Black and white photographs (the result would have been no different if they had been in color) were ingeniously arranged in cartoon panel sequences to tell the story of the hapless birdmen. It didn't work. A number of flyers had occasion to use

James Ensor

Uffizi, Florence

Ben Shahn

their pictorial passports, but the natives seldom had any idea what the small black and white images meant. Never having seen the flat, reduced images in photographs they were incapable of translating their meaning. The military establishments with all their experts had overlooked one fundamental fact: We do not carry in our genes the inherent ability to understand photo images. It is a *learned* capacity.

In our society everyone who can see is exposed to a vast variety of pictures almost from the first blink at the glaring lights in the maternity ward. Photographs, books, magazines, newspapers, television, and movies are so common, so pervasive, we fail to recognize their apparently automatic assimilation. We tend to think of such material as part of natural vision. But as knowledgeable missionaries and other travelers to out-of-the-way places could have told the Army, if you are not educated to *see* photographs they are quite *unnatural* and meaningless.

Nor is this kind of perceptual problem restricted to primitive people. Pictures vary from culture to culture. With today's omnipresent communications—mechanical picture representations bouncing off satellites to receivers in every

To the untutored observer these typical newspaper photographs would appear incomprehensible. If you had never seen a photo, let alone rocking chairs, eyeglasses, neckties, and microphones, it would be difficult to understand these strange fragmented images.

Which portrait is more real? The answer all depends on who is doing the looking, and how they are conditioned to what they see.

corner of the world—vast numbers of people have become versed in translating printed and electronic images. This has not always been the case.

Consider this documented experience of a British naval expedition while visiting China in the latter part of the eighteenth century. On meeting the Chinese emperor the British commander offered a portrait of his sovereign, King George the Third, as a gift to his host. The oil painting was a three-quarter view, handsomely rendered in the chiaroscuro manner of the day.

The emperor was shocked. Had the king a deformed eye, and did he suffer from a disease that discolored so much of his face? After hearing assurances that King George was sound of wind and limb and the portrait was a perfect likeness, the emperor showed his guests his own portrait. It was printed in Oriental style, a frontal view with flat overall lighting. The painter had made no attempt to suggest the illusion of depth or volume, nor were there disquieting shadows causing a discolored complexion. It was to the emperor's eye a realistic representation of his divine radiance.

Obviously there is more to seeing than meets the eye. We see and comprehend in accordance with our conditioning. Physiologically we all see things in a similar way, but how we perceive and interpret them can be far different. Even when we are of like background and comparable training we still bring to the subject our own unique emotional and intellectual gestalt.

Closure and projection

Two other phenomena of seeing are of special significance to artists. These are usually referred to as the *closure* and *projection* principles. To one degree or another, all of us have a tendency to complete lines and patterns when they are not shown. Our visual/mental apparatus seems to abhor incompleteness. Shown in the margin is an example of how the artist can use the closure principle to involve the viewer's imagination to supply the missing areas. Rembrandt is noted for his frequent and masterful use of this approach.

In a similar vein, projection is the habit of our inner eye to form recognizable images from almost any amorphous elements we encounter, be they cumulus clouds, cracks in the ceiling plaster, or inkblots. (The latter, under the name Rorschach test, is a standard tool of psychologists to help discover a patient's subconscious stimuli.)

Around five hundred years ago Leonardo da Vinci made these notes about projection: "It may seem trifling and almost laughable [yet it] is nevertheless extremely useful in assisting

Marc Chagall *Stedelijk Museum, Amsterdam*

Austin Briggs

the mind to find variety for composition. By looking attentively at old and stained walls, or stones and veined marble of various colors, you may fancy that you see in them several compositions, landscapes, battles, figures in quick motion, strange countenances, and dresses, with an infinity of other objects. By these confused lines [you can] find any name or word you choose to imagine."

Surely the artist can conjure up more than simply recording what he sees. Let the camera do that job. In visually expressing what excites us we can paint the familiar with relentless fidelity, or we can zoom into our inner psyche and invent unknown worlds. And whether responding to what we see in the real world or inventing something altogether new, we bring to our interpretation a personal point of view to add to the beholder's perception and understanding. In this manner our visualizations, in whatever form, serve as expressions that communicate to others something not previously known or understood. At such times the products of our efforts have meaning and purpose.

Closure principle — our mind's eye rejects incompleteness.

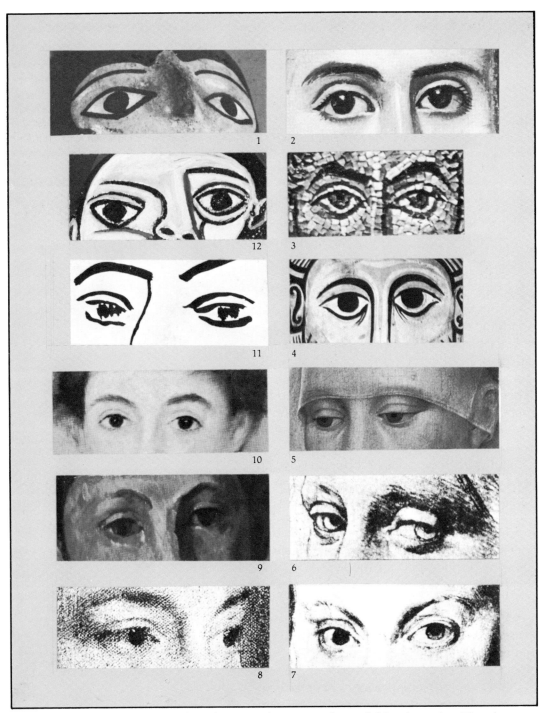

Eyes, as conceived by artists throughout the ages, make an expressive symbol for observation. They also reveal a variety of individual interpretations, as well as cultural influences. Notice the evolutionary circle leading clockwise from the primitive around 100 B.C. back toward the primitive approach of modern times. Details by 1, Unknown Nazca Indian, Peru; 2, Unknown Egyptian; 3, Unknown Roman (mosaic); 4, Unknown Frenchman; 5, Rogier van der Weyden, Flemish; 6, Leonardo da Vinci, Italian; 7, Peter Paul Rubens, Flemish; 8, Edgar Degas, French; 9, Paul Cézanne, French; 10, Pièrre Renoir, French; 11, Henri Matisse, French; 12, Pablo Picasso, Spanish.

A variety of approaches

Artists and people interested in art are usually quite capable of reading, but most of us would rather spend our time looking at pictures. A book primarily addressing such an audience should emphasize the *show* rather than the *tell*. Such will be the approach for the remainder of the section. Demonstrations and examples are of particular value when dealing with material as slippery to grasp as a wet fish. Surely the formation of ideas and the understanding of picture concept fit such a category.

The examples of picture ideas and concept that follow have been culled from a variety of artists. Each offers his own approach to specific problems. From these specifics you may be able to discern a procedure that you can adapt to your own uses; at least, you may gain a better insight into the thinking behind each of the compositions. As much as possible, the words used in describing the pictures and the process are those of the artists. They have been compiled from notes, letters, interviews, taped and written accounts, as well as recollections of talks, discussions and personal observation.

When viewing the examples of preliminary work keep in mind that an experienced artist performs an amalgam of functions seemingly simultaneously. All of the artists whose work is shown have considerable mastery of all phases of picture making, and each one utilizes these skills in different ways at different stages. For many, very rough, suggestive sketches and abstract compositional indications are all they need to substantiate the salient picture shapes and values. Do not be misled as to the importance of the procedure because of the crude, simplistic sketches. This thinking process is the basis of the picture, but was never intended for the eyes of others. Also, because of the apparent haste with which these unpolished roughs have been produced, do not conclude the *thinking* and *planning* were cut short in any way. Indeed, many times the thinking stage takes longer and requires more effort than completing the final rendering.

You will notice that not every artist approaches the problem in the same way. For some the natural way of working calls for more explicit sketches, while most need only the simplest suggestions, and some can seemingly dispense with almost all of the initial visual representation. Others may do their planning by loosely painting in color. In any case, you can be sure composition, drawing, value patterns, color, and all other pictorial considerations are never out of mind as the groping for picture concept proceeds. Your method of working may be quite different. That is of no consequence. *How* you go about solving your problem is not important. Understanding the thinking process is what counts.

Implications contain more intrigue to the eye and the spirit than exposition. Suggestions insinuate more than a final statement could ever produce. In short, a good sketch is a promise that if everything goes well the final emotional and intellectual haul will be colossal. But it stops right at the promise and leaves fulfillment to the imagination. Thus, the sketch stimulates phantasies and expectations.

Frederic Taubes (1900-1981)

Norman Rockwell

"Getting good ideas is always a problem. It takes a lot of digging. I do lots of doodling and make rough kinds of cartoon sketches on cheap paper. Sometimes I draw a blank for hours, but I keep at it. When I get discouraged I stop—go for a walk, a bike ride, or look at books and magazines. Coming back at it after a delay I may find a good idea rather quickly.

"How do you know when you get a good idea? You'll know. For me, bells start to ring and I want to start painting right away. It is best to keep plugging until you know you have a good idea. A picture will never be better than the idea. To persist with a mediocre one wastes time, and the picture will be mediocre, too.[1]

"Fine pictures can come from ordinary human experiences. Usually simple things. What I have trouble with are the big, earth-shaking ideas. They are beyond me. I must say what I want to say in terms of ordinary people in everyday situations. I find I can fit anything into that frame, even big ideas like freedom of speech or freedom of worship.[2]

"Putting across a picture idea is like throwing a ball against a wall—it comes back at you with less force than you threw it. From a realistic point of view this means you always have to exaggerate every idea, pose and action to carry the idea with the force you want. And, of course, it must be in just the right setting."

Rockwell's search for picture ideas (opposite page) always started the same way: He drew a lamppost. "I must start somewhere," he said, "and if I did not start with the lamppost or something else, I would spend the day looking at blank paper."[3] By association of ideas the lamppost next acquired a not-so-sober sailor. The sailor brought to mind the fact men aboard ship must do their own mending. This led to thoughts of mother at home, and at home there was always a dog. "As Jack Atherton used to tell me," Rockwell said, "every picture I do ends up with a Boy Scout, a dog and the American flag. I guess that's the way my mind works."[1]

The sequence progresses with the idea of the dog being sick, taking him to a doctor . . . doctors lead to thoughts of a pretty girl sick in bed . . . why was she sick . . . she caught a cold at a square dance . . . and she had danced so much her shoes needed repairing. Not a bad idea, Rockwell thought, but Steve Dohanos recently did a shoemaker cover. Darn. Things are getting desperate. Better luck tomorrow.

1 From notes taken at instructors' meeting at the Famous Artists School.
2 Famous Artists Magazine, Vol. 8, No. 3, 1960
3 How I Make a Picture *by Norman Rockwell*
© 1949 *Institute of Commercial Art/R.D. Cortina Co., Inc.*

Rockwell's search for picture ideas followed an evolutionary course.

YANKEE DOODLE CAME TO TOWN · RIDING ON A PONY · S

Preliminary sketch for the Yankee Doodle mural.

"When they asked me to do a mural for the Nassau Tavern I had some doubts about it. I had never done a mural before and the size, thirteen feet long by about five feet high, was a little scary. There was never much concern about the idea. Princeton was so important historically during the Revolution it just seemed automatic to do Yankee Doodle.

"Also, I never had much doubt about the point of view. I usually see a scene as if it is going by me on a stage. In a lot of ways I think of what I do as if I were a stage director. I get excited about finding just the right props and costumes. I was intrigued with the uniforms and the research here—the costumes are all authentic and some were especially made for the painting.

"You'll notice I relied on the old stunt of playing straight, rigid forms against moving ones—the boy in front of the soldier at the window; the kid holding the pony's tail in front of the doorway; the woman with her hands on her hips against the cavorting redcoats . . . . In a picture everything depends on variety.

"I worked a little differently than normal on this picture. Usually I call in models and photograph them in natural positions they assume under my direction. In this case I did this sketch (above) first and then got the models to adapt to the

34

UCK A FEATHER IN HIS HAT · AND CALLED IT MACARONI

The finished mural as it appears at the Nassau Inn, Princeton, New Jersey.

sketch. It didn't work too well. As Howard Pyle said, 'The artist should climb over the frame of the picture and become one with the characters he is painting.' I should have done more of that here."[1]

1 From notes taken at instructor meetings at the Famous Artists School

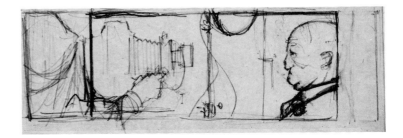

Joseph Hirsch

"A stranger once asked me if I was in the entertainment world; I almost said yes, but I thought of my paintings and said, 'No, I make cudgels.' Such self-righteousness makes me squirm, but it is a discomfort I live with. It is not easy to stay out of step."[1]

As an artist Joe Hirsch was preoccupied with interpreting the human figure realistically. As a successful gallery painter during the zenith of American nonobjective painting he often felt he was marching to the sound of a different drummer. Most of his life he lived in large cities. He was an astute and sometimes sardonic observer of the human condition. Many of the ideas for his pictures followed an evolutionary course from chance encounter to a quick and fertile association of ideas. The result was often overlaid with a mantle of humor and satire, along with sympathetic bows to human dignity.

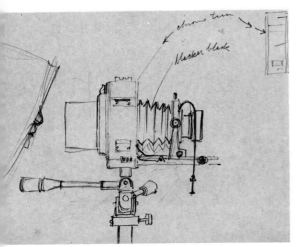

"The alert eye every day can catch hundreds of glimpses, any one of which might serve as the seed of a possible picture. For centuries the whole tradition of sketchbooks, in which artists store these seeds while the memory is fresh, has been based on the validity of brief revelations of glimpses."[2]

On these pages are a few of Joe's recollections showing how a painting can result from a chance glance.

"While a photographer was taking some pictures in my studio, I became intrigued by the bellows of his camera. I made these quick sketches, took a few liberties and sometime later produced the painting." [Shown below.]

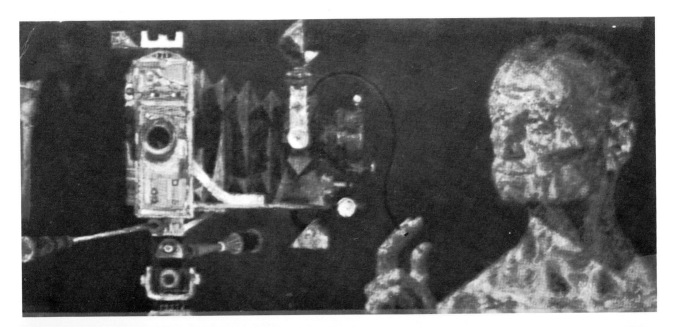

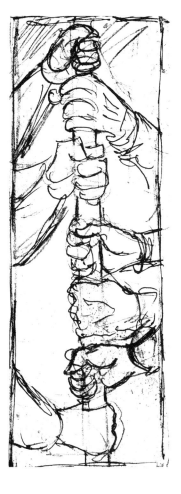

"It is only a guess on my part that there is a connection between the sketch of the many hands holding the pole [at the left] and the finished painting [above]. A more direct connection might exist, conceivably, between the many images of Christ bearing the cross, to which any young, museum-hunting art student is exposed, and my bearded fellow with the slight smile. I think the above face, partly obscured by the glaringly white pole, may well be more interesting than if all the features were entirely exposed. Here a gratuitous confession; after, and only after, the painting was signed and framed did it occur to me that the man merited a monocle."[2]

1 Written by Mr. Hirsch for a catalog of his paintings exhibited at the Forum Gallery, New York City, in 1969.
2 Excerpted from notes and letters from the artist to the author, portions of which were used in an article for the Famous Artists Magazine, *Vol.18, No. 3, 1970.*

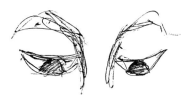

"It started with this downward cast of the eyes. The idea likely came from someone I observed on a bus or subway."

A number of Joe Hirsch's pictures deal with engaging characters who may dwell somewhat outside the confines of the real world. Joe has a fondness for nymphs. He often placed them in diabolic situations. These sketches with his words describe the sequence of his picture idea development.

"Before I had even started to sketch I had in mind the idea of the nymph painting a sinister, leering face. This is my initial try. The big face's nose and the mouth are too evident. In an effort to enlarge the nymph I lowered the top edge. Always good to try moving picture limits to heighten, shorten, or widen areas."

"Should she be on a ladder or scaffold and wearing shoes? No, it adds nothing to the basic notion, nor to the decorative form."

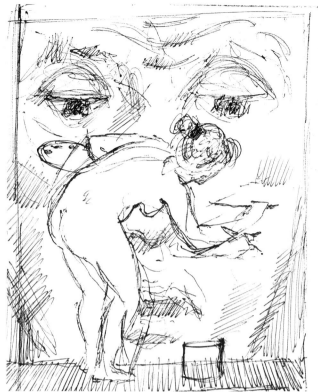

"The bending figure was better, I decided, because it was less monumental. And the entire figure was a more striking contrast to the big scale portion of the physiognomy."

"Would a standing figure be preferable? Showing feet and/or legs? or cut at mid-thigh? I ask these questions in this rough sketch and feel the answer to be No."

"This face seems here too naturalistic and the nymph too small. Also, if she's to be light-skinned against the dark face, her hair should be more lost against a dark background."

"The sketch above was done on-the-spot along the French Mediterranean coast. The two smaller sketches were done later and are concerned with the dark and light values of the three horizontal bands of sky, sea, and sand.

"I chose to emphasize the lightness of the beach, as the 'finished' painting indicates. The sea and sky are much more fused than in the sketches, the horizon only suggested softly. On seeing the painting exhibited publicly I realized that I had led myself astray with a concern for treating sky, sea, and sand with landscape importance, for wondering about the horizon's sharpness or softness. I had forgotten the fresh impact the motorcyles had when I first saw the mechanical couple because I did not stress it in my on-the-spot sketch, namely, the big, heavy still life on rubber and steel, bristling with gadgets, dark against the glare of the sunlit context.

"Accordingly, back in the studio, I reworked the painting to conform with the one dominant thought of an isolated bouquet of machinery. All the bathers save one are gone, the driftwood is minimized, the horizon obliterated, the lower eye-level giving a more looming quality to the vehicles. The completed picture, right, finished for the second time is fairly well the way I want it. The Danish philosopher Kierkegaard put great value on having *one thought only*. In painting it is disastrous to give equal importance to a number of things at the expense of the *one* overall theme."

Famous Artists Magazine, Vol. 18, No. 3, 1970

Painting as first exhibited.

Reworked final version.

Robert Fawcett

The illustrator, Bob Fawcett, called his search for picture ideas "an act of ruminating." He would doodle on anything at hand from envelopes to odd scraps of Strathmore or Whatman board, using his currently favored drawing instrument. This varied almost daily, from large soft lead pencils to pliable felt markers to ruling pens. Whatever he drew with, his doodling was done almost unconsciously while his mind concentrated on the story—its subject, characters, setting, and general mood.

As things progressed, one after another of his marks would suggest new images. Rough sketches would begin to emerge. Out of the abstract some shapes and forms became recognizable, and the artist's inner eye would react and move the elements in that direction. From these, other images would become apparent. The procedure was repeated over and over. He would hold onto an abstract approach as long as possible so, as he said, "the germination of ideas would have full rein."

After many tries a definite picture idea would slowly present itself. Only when satisfied he had the right point of view, the right angle and the general placement of the major forms and shapes, would he start to compose the picture at a larger scale. Even then, as can be seen in the sequence of sketches shown on the following pages, the shifting and adjusting continued.

Robert Fawcett was known and admired for his draftsmanship, but he often admitted the most exciting time for him in creating a picture was the abstract concept stage. "This is the way I swing the golf club," he would say. "You have to do it your way. One thing is certain; how well you learn to hit the ball will depend on practice."

Above are a few of Fawcett's rough, abstract doodles which eventually evolved into the illustration of Leonardo in the process of painting the Mona Lisa. The sketch at the right, as well as those on the following pages show Fawcett's search for the final composition after he had established the concept.

One of many near-final versions in pencil.

An example of one of Fawcett's idea sketches drawn
a ruling pen.

Final sketch done on tracing paper.

Ben Shahn

Although his work may be described as more symbolic and intellectual than realistic, Shahn often mentioned that the point of departure for everything he did was based on first-hand experience. "Art," he said, "has its roots in real life . . . life itself, as it chances to exist, furnishes the stimulus for art."

A keen and articulate observer of the passing scene, Ben was fascinated with the paradoxes and contrasts of what he saw. Social comment, coupled with humor and pathos, is often apparent in his work. The preliminary sketches shown here suggest his approach.

While attending a watermelon festival at a state fair, Shahn was taken by the color and the busy, animated environment of the setting. The scene seemed to suggest a number of picture possibilities. He explored the subject with rough, on-the-spot sketches, some of which are shown at the top of the opposite page. Additional explorations were made later in his studio.

Almost from the start Shahn found his interest concentrating on a portly gentleman who was totally absorbed in the subject at hand. Experimenting continued, searching for just the right pose, gesture of the hands, sizes and positions of the pieces of watermelon, as well as the patterns on the shirt, tablecloth and the background. Many alterations and refinements are evident in the final painting, but the character and thrust of the original sketches are clearly evident.

Final painting

Unlike many so-called fine artists (*gallery artist* seems a more appropriate title), Shahn frequently undertook illustration assignments. This preliminary work, done to illustrate a story for a popular national magazine, was about a child in a playground. Visiting such a scene near his home in Roosevelt, New Jersey, the artist searched for revealing information. Again he was drawn to the contrasts of the human condition. Along with dozens of rough-and-ready kids enjoying the give-and-take of robust activities, Shahn noted the lonely, left-out children who were shunted to the sidelines.

The search for just the right props and other elements keyed to the artist's personal approach is evident in these roughs. It is from these idea sketches that the concept for the final picture evolved.

Al Parker

Someone once asked Al Parker if he ever painted for fun. "Oh," Al responded, "I always enjoy what I do."

"That's not what I mean," the questioner continued. "What do you paint for yourself when you are not working on a specific assignment?"

Al looked nonplussed, then replied, "I don't. I get my kicks from solving the client's problems."

And that Alfred Charles Parker has been doing with style for about fifty years. Few illustrators enjoy such respect of their peers. No less an authority than Norman Rockwell called him the greatest influence on American illustration since Howard Pyle. How did Parker, a frustrated jazz musician from St. Louis, garner such a reputation? Surely a number of his colleagues could draw, paint, and design as well as he, but hardly any could match his popularity or longevity in a business noted for fickleness. The answer is simple: Al Parker is the consummate pictorial innovator. He *thinks*; he conceives each illustration anew. He is not content to rely on a formula or to repeat previously proven concepts and viewpoints. This is the way Al describes his approach.

"I always try to avoid the stereotyped, hackneyed arrangement. I pretend I am seeing the figures and props for the first time and discard any preconceived ideas about them. The ordinary arrangement is not an eye catcher, but sometimes a simple twist or turn can make it one. It is these little things that lift an illustration out of dullsville.

"All the problems should be solved at the rough stage. I often sketch the actual size the finished art will appear in the magazine. Research is important. Finding just the right prop is often the clue to the composition. There is no need to labor over the rough. Save the rendering for the finish, otherwise you get tired before it is done. My roughs are simple and rather abstract. Most of the placement is done almost unconsciously. At this stage it is all forms and shapes, not specifics. The placement and weight help set the mood. The better the forms are placed, the more pleasing the arrangement, the more the viewer will be attracted."[1]

1 *How I Make a Picture* by Al Parker
© 1949 Institute of Commercial Art/R.D. Cortina Co., Inc.

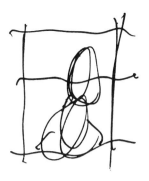

These are the kinds of abstract roughs Parker would develop as the conceptual basis for his illustrations. Below is a black and white reproduction of the picture as it appeared in the American Weekly.

Claude Croney

The popular watercolorist and workshop teacher, Claude Croney, has this to say about the search for picture ideas: "Many people [when painting scenery] do panoramas as an easy way to avoid making decisions. Yet the success of most painting depends on how the artist edits and selects from what he sees. Students think the professional painter starts and ends in just the right place—without making any mistakes in between. That's hardly the case.

"The preliminary sketch is the germ of the idea. It helps me decide whether or not the subject has a chance . . . . There is no point in doing big sketches. Small thumbnails will let you see what won't work, and then you can move on to another idea.

"When I'm sure of what I want to do, I draw freely and then panel off a promising area. I look for value patterns and interesting shapes. Looking at these sketches, nobody but myself would be able to understand them. It is my own special shorthand."[1]

1 From the manuscript for the book, *Croney on Watercolor*; text by Charles Movalli, published by North Light, © 1981.

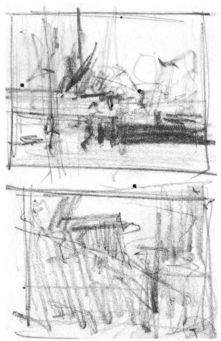

This idea was developed from the abstract shapes the artist saw in a portion of a newspaper photograph of a group of young hockey players.

The preliminary sketch on which the final painting is based. It is reproduced actual size.

Reproduction of the completed watercolor

Bob Peak

A few years back Bob Peak was quoted as saying: "For me, *now* is the thing. I need something immediate—fast materials to work with and quick results." Sometime later he exuberantly exclaimed he had rediscovered the joys of oil painting. "What a kick," he said, "to stand in front of a big canvas and swing a big brush like the old boys."[1] Whatever his approach, Bob produces great quantities of work, all of which is marked with a style and a quality that have made him one of the nation's most successful illustrators.

On a number of occasions I visited Bob while he was at work in his studio. Interrupt is probably a more apt word, as he was always rushing to meet a deadline. What a fascinating workplace it was, full of gear and materials with mountains of drawings and paintings in various stages of completion piled everywhere. From the coveys of pigeons in the courtyard to the festooning cobwebs on the dusty stairway, Bob's old warehouse studio looked like a setting Woody Allen might invent for a film about a dedicated illustrator.

It is interesting to reflect that in all my visits I never recall seeing amidst the clutter any rough sketches or diagrams such as those developed by most of the other artists discussed in this section. It is possible Bob makes them, but it doesn't seem likely. He goes at things his own way. He apparently can conceptualize his picture ideas without much recourse to the usual preliminary procedures. He seems to have the ability to formulate his mind's eye image by designing with reference material directly from a Balopticon projection. The sketch at the left shows the kind of drawing Bob would probably classify as preliminary.

All of this is not to suggest that this artist relies exclusively on mechanical means to achieve his pictures. Quite the contrary. He does a great deal of thinking about each job. Before starting any picture he says he considers these questions: "What is the problem and how can I solve it? Who is the audience? What experience do I have with the subject? What materials should I use and what is the best style for the job?"

An interviewer once asked how he kept from being influenced by the advertising and magazine art he sees. Peak replied: "I'm a closet artist. I prefer to work out my own problems in my own style with only the kind of influence I seek out. Long ago I learned it is best to go back into art histo-

1 Conversation with the author

Notice in the preliminary drawing above how the action and mood are emphasized. At this stage Peak's emotional involvement is apparent. The sketch at the right shows another step in the search for the best solution to the problem. Below is the illustration as it was published.

ry and find something to use. By the time you have imitated something current it is out-of-date. The style that used to last for five years is now lucky if it's good for two years. You must keep your style a fluid thing."[2]

At one point Bob was much taken with the work of the Austrian painter, Gustav Klimt. The Peak illustrations of the period showed a strong Art Nouveau influence, although with modifications and variations. At the time, Bob was asked what he would think of Klimt's approach if the artist were alive and working today. Without a pause, he shot back, "It would be old hat."

Peak's procedures and fluidity work for him. The inexperienced practitioner, however, would be wise to proceed on this path with caution. There is much more to achieving the B. Peak *look* than researching past styles and learning to manipulate mechanical drawing devices.

Austin Briggs

Bud Briggs earned his living as an illustrator. He was good at it, but it always struck me that he was a frustrated painter. Unlike Parker, Peak, and a number of others, he never seemed truly satisfied with solving other people's picture problems. This was a puzzle because he approached an illustration in much the way he would if he were working strictly to satisfy his own aesthetic urges. Possibly this was one of the factors in his success.

"It is the business of the artist," he wrote, "to see the common everyday experiences of people in a new and fresh way, and to show them as if they were being presented for the first time. Since each of us is a unique individual, if we are truly aware of our experiences and the world in which these experiences take place, we cannot help presenting the old theme in a fresh way. Unfortunately, most of us tend to see things through others' eyes. We relate our own special experiences to the standard experience pattern of our fellows, and for this reason we tend to fall into the cliché.

"Most successful pictures deal with basic human feelings and experiences. Beginning artists often feel such themes are trite. They are—in the sense that they are the common experience of humanity. The more trite the basic theme of your picture the better. The cliché to worry about is the *visual* cliché. Search for subtle variations which present the old theme in a new light. Comedians know the truth of the saying, 'An old joke is the best joke . . . it is all in how you tell it.' "[1]

The examples shown on these pages suggest the artist's way of stalking what he considered the best solution.

1 *How I Make a Picture* by Austin Briggs
© 1952 Institute of Commercial Art/R.D. Cortina Co., Inc.

This story had to do with a boy whose arm was paralyzed for some time. He becomes angry and resentful about the moral misdeeds of his mother and he hits her. In that instant the mental block that caused the paralysis disappears and he is able to move his arm again. The illustration problem was to concentrate attention on two things: the boy's hand, and the cringing figure of the woman.

In this sketch the woman is not important enough.

Better, but the two important ideas are not clear.

Now the woman's prominence is better, but the hand is still not successful.

This seemed to be the best solution. The lighting allowed both the boy's hand and the woman's face to be emphasized. This is the way the final illustration appeared in Cosmopolitan magazine.

Sketches with permission of R.D. Cortina Co., Inc. © 1952

Oskar Kokoschka, Emil Nolde

Possibly it is a needless non sequitur to include in this roster of more or less representational American artists, two European painters of a decidedly different artistic persuasion. Although difficult to classify, both Nolde and Kokoschka are generally grouped among the so-called "wild Moderns" known as German Expressionists. There is a twofold purpose in introducing them here: first, to broaden the base for considering the validity of the kind of conceptual thinking under discussion; and second, to suggest there might be a kinship in the way a wide variety of artists employ the subconscious flow of abstract thinking in their search for picture ideas.

Emil Nolde

Oskar Kokoschka

Unfortunately, I had no firsthand association with either artist. However, their writings offer some insight into their thinking. For the painter, "instinct is ten times what knowledge is," wrote Nolde. From all accounts, the artist frequently relied on images accumulated in and released from his subconscious. Most of his colorful paintings (see page 191) seemed to spring from the depths of his psyche.

In a letter to his fiancée in 1901 Nolde wrote: "I was standing there painting two small houses, their outlines indistinct in the sunset, peaceful behind the dunes. The wind began to blow, the clouds grew wild and dark, a storm blew up, and grayish sand whirled high above the dunes and the houses. A raging storm—then, suddenly, my brush ripped through the canvas. I came back to myself. I looked around me: the sunset was still beautiful and calm; I had lived through a storm in my imagination and been carried away . . . ."

Emil Nolde

In a similar though less emotional vein, Kokoschka said this: "Consciousness is the cause of all things, including conceptions; it is a sea whose horizons are things seen . . . . Consciousness is the grave of things, the point at which they come to an end. So that as they end they seem no longer to consist of anything more existent than my vision within myself . . . . Things will come to act on my behalf and admit themselves of their own accord; I have spoken in your stead with my vision. My spirit has spoken!"

Although the intonations and results are individual and different in final form, it seems many artists approach picture making from a common ground. Toward the end of this section we will consider additional examples on this theme by examining some preliminary sketches of artists from earlier periods.

Emil Nolde

Oskar Kokoschka

Ben Stahl

The career of Ben Stahl runs the gamut from top-notch illustrator to prize-winning gallery painter—and a great deal in between. Whatever he tackles he does so with gusto and much emotion.

Ben abhors the growing dependency on photography evident in the works of so many contemporary artists who work in the realm of realism.* "When you compose your picture through the ground glass of a camera," he says, "the result is neither a good drawing, a good painting, nor even a good photograph." Art is life to Ben Stahl, and life would not be worth living if controlled by formulas, dogmatic procedures, and machines. "Pictures to be worth a damn must have feeling," he admonishes. "They must grow out of the artist's involvement and reactions to life."

"Injecting life and spirit into a painting is not easy. You must keep yourself free and flexible all through the drawing and painting process. Try to avoid preconceived ideas and rigid preliminary sketches. Once you pin down a composition into frozen forms the chance of giving the final painting some kind of vitality is small. Creativity comes from tapping your subconscious. Work to let the inspiration you feel find its way out as unhindered as possible. We must breathe life into our work all at once. It is an impulsive, immediate action."[1]

How does the artist accomplish all this? Since there is no formula to follow, no blow-by-blow description can be documented. However, as these sketches suggest, a pattern of testing, exploring, refinement, and development is evident that warrants the attention of the serious observer.

1 Excerpts of letters from the artist to the author
* *Always a paradox, Ben confided he has recently discovered how useful the instant camera can be in helping to solve fold and drapery problems. He is also excited about a new pint-size Balopticon that he uses to enlarge his roughs.*

"Based on observed and remembered poses, I explored and searched for actions and attitudes of characters you would find in an old western saloon. Not much conscious thought here. I just tried to stay loose and flexible."

"Here you can see how the characters from the previous page found their way into this more finished charcoal drawing. The dance hall Dolly turned up in this and other poses in other pictures."

"These are all thinking sketches—the search for picture ideas."

Above, an early concept sketch that eventually evolved into a number of compositions. One of the finished drawings is shown below.

Ben Stahl

Ben Stahl

"It is fun and often rewarding to explore ideas in color. Keep loose and fluid. Sometimes great things happen you could never plan."

Albin Henning

"Most of the stories assigned to me are full of action. There is never much question about the best part to illustrate. The scene jumps out at you from the manuscript as you read it. The important thing is to work out the right feeling for the story as a whole. It always bothers me when an artist illustrates some obscure action that has little bearing on the essence of the story. It seems unfair to the reader. In most cases, the fault probably rests with the editors—many have a knack for picking the wrong scene. Being word-oriented they like the way the words are put together, but the passage may have little visual appeal.

"This preliminary sketch (above) was done in oil on the back of an old envelope. The story was about the Russian Revolution. As I read the manuscript I noted the caption (at the right) that seemed to set the stage and explain all the action to follow. I wanted to capture a feeling of movement and impending violence and hold it all in a somber, yet violent key. The Russian Revolution was a wild, confused, brutal affair that always carries a sense of mystery, at least, so it seems to most of us in this country. In many ways I think the sketch captures that kind of feeling. In fact, as with many roughs, it does the job somewhat better than the final picture which had to be more boiled-out and detailed.

"I often do preliminary roughs directly in oil like this because it helps to solve the tonal problem. If you get the tones along with the general movement right, you establish the *spirit*. Then you can play around with the composition and the figures. Usually you can make them work without much trouble. As Dunn said: 'Pictures must be held together with spirit.' He was right.[1]

1 These statements are not really direct quotations, but they are based on memories of talks with my father, and though the exact sequence of words may be questioned, the meaning, thrust, and flavor of the remarks cannot be challenged.

These sailing ship scenes were sketches in search of the right concept for an illustration dealing with a historic battle at sea. They were done in opaque watercolor. Although the subjects shown on these pages all deal with strong, action-packed events, notice the differences in the moods suggested. All of these sketches are reproduced at the same size they were painted.

"If an illustrator is given a good story to work with he seldom has much trouble finding episodes that will make good pictures. Trouble usually stems from editors or art directors sticking their noses into areas they should leave to the artist. In the long run, the editors will get better illustrations and have a finer looking book if they let the artist alone. All the illustrator needs to know is the number of pictures required, and if there are any production restrictions concerning color, size, and the like.

"These sketches were made for a story that appeared in *The Saturday Evening Post*. It was about a young fellow from a small backwoods town who went off to the city and made it big. He went back home on a visit as a real city slicker. There wasn't much action—the main thing of interest was the dude's visit to the village's old general store. It had a big potbellied stove and was the town's main gathering place.

"I knew right away the store scene was the thing to illustrate. It had the right atmosphere, and the different characters could supply interest. Also, all those things you'd find in old stores—stove, spittoon, cracker barrels, et cetera—would be good to use in the composition. As I worked on the rough color sketch I felt there should be a warm light coming through the windows. I hadn't planned it that way at first, but it established a good mood and made for strong silhouetted shapes which helped give emphasis to the characters.

"The final picture when reproduced was well received, but there are things about the sketch I like better.

This is the finished illustration as it appeared in The Saturday Evening Post.

"These are the roughs I did for a story about a squad of soldiers in the jungle who had to run the gauntlet down a narrow river, the shores of which were controlled by hundreds of hostile natives. The Legionnaires mounted a machine gun on their sampan-type craft, but they still had a hell of a time getting through because the natives were armed with poisoned spears and arrows.

"The entire story was about the fight, so there was not much doubt about what to illustrate. The only question was, from whose side should you view the action? It seemed to me a close-up view of the boat was best. When guns and shooting are the main part of a story, it is best to be honest and put the emphasis on them. Since the natives wouldn't be seen easily from the river, reader interest, I thought, might be generated by curiosity over what all the shooting was about. A vignetted shape also seemed to add something to the general excitement and mystery.

"For the illustrator, all these considerations are important. After all, the whole purpose of the picture is to get people to read the story. You have to think about these things from the beginning.

"As you can see, I first made a couple of rough concept sketches and then solved most of the problems in the oil sketch. In this case I made the sketch the same size it appeared when reproduced in the magazine. The finished illustration looked pretty much the same, but it lost some of the punch."

Fritz Henning

For more than forty years the local residents and the summer folk at Lake Winnipesaukee, New Hampshire, have hailed the daily passages of the *M. V. Mount Washington* as she negotiates her thirty-mile course from the Weirs to Wolfeboro and on down to Alton Bay. For families such as ours who have enjoyed a long association with *The Lake,* sighting the "Mount" is part of the scene and one of the ways we keep track of time.

About ten o'clock most summer mornings the 205-foot vessel passes the Bear Island post office dock just prior to making a wide turn between Pine and Three Mile Islands and heading down the channel toward Center Harbor. It is an impressive sight that always generates a strong sense of movement, speed, and drama as the ship passes close aboard at cruising speed. It is this feeling I hoped to capture and record. From a concept point of view the problem was to take this slice of reality and, with editing and modifications, mold it into a picture to express a sensation of an event rather than a factual recording of it.

The roughs shown on the opposite page suggest the evolution of the thinking that occurred. The first few sketches show the scene more or less as it exists with the building on the right side of the dock. This positioning didn't work. It failed to convey the explosive effect you get as the vessel, passing from left to right, is suddenly abeam and close enough so the slap of the propellers and the throb of the diesels are part of the experience. Shifting the structure to the left margin and bringing the ship closer helped.

The sketch in opaque watercolor above solved most of the problems. In fact, I like it better than the finished painting shown at the bottom of the opposite page. What went wrong? The final rendering misses the mark, mainly because I became too involved in making an accurate portrait of the ship. As a result, the *spirit* of the picture—the feeling of movement and drama—suffered.

Paul Landry

"My children love to walk on rock walls," comments this fine landscape and marine painter. "For a happy memory of these days, I wanted to incorporate that idea [in a painting]."

Paul's initial idea for the picture is shown below. It is reproduced the same size as originally drawn. The small roughs on the opposite page show how the artist explored a number of variations. "You can't be content with your first concept," he continues. "You have to adjust, rearrange, reconsider."

In the exploratory sketches the artist was concerned only with shapes, line and the placement of the forms in relation to the picture space. He says he often does fifteen or twenty such arrangements, always searching for new visual possibilities. Notice how he has shifted the point of view and moved the shapes and dominant lines in his effort to find the right balance and feeling of movement.

From all these roughs the best solutions are selected and refined. Only then is thought given to the details of the major elements. More probing is done to refine the design possibilities of such objects as the trees, the barn, and the wall so they will work well in the final composition. These preliminary thinking steps, the artist feels, are most important to the development of a good picture.[1]

1 Sketches from Landry's book, *On Drawing and Painting,* published by North Light, ©1977

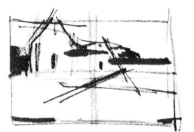

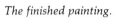

The finished painting.

John McDermott

McDermott was a colorful character and a specialist in almost everything. Most of the time he concentrated on illustration, a career at which he earned moderate success. He also wrote a couple of novels. But most of all he was captivated by making movies . . . backyard, 16mm sound films of battles. With the help of many friends (mainly as actors) he wrote the scripts, planned the scenes, unearthed the costumes, and operated the camera and sound equipment. He also cut and edited the finished film.

His idea was to document battles the way the soldiers involved saw and felt them. They were tough, they were real. One, an episode about Pickett's charge in the Civil War, found its way to national television. However, most of John's films have never been seen. They were, John thought, too raw and powerful for general audiences to appreciate.

McDermott knew about war as he knew about drawing and visualizing picture concepts. This is how he described his experience during World War II: "In the Marines as a combat artist, I traveled with the troops and for three years got all the drawing opportunity anyone could want. My work changed enormously during this time and I'm sure it was due to constant drawing every single day from life. No photographs, no copying somebody's historical painting. Just putting down what I saw around me. In a few instances it was a dangerous kind of scholarship, but it was the nearest I ever had to an unrelieved stint of drawing."[1]

The sketches and notes shown here are the kind of story boards John made to plan a filming sequence. This movie was about a battle in World War I. Visualizing ideas to be translated to film takes the same kind of conceptual thinking necessary to create any picture. John put it this way: "To me, painting, writing and making films are merely different means of achieving the same result—the communication of an idea. An illustration must say it all in one picture; a novel can take chapters and build toward a finish; a film is a happy combination of all of it—pictures, story line, cutting for effect and sound. I always found the three fields to be not all that far apart."[1]

1 North Light, Vol. 5, No. 3, 1973

"Jumps over camera"

"a guy crosses in front at 'same as ever'"

"comin' up here no more today"

"he walks straight into camera"

← Pan

(SMOKE)
B.G.

Earlier artists

Most of the examples of picture concept procedures we have examined so far have centered on artists of the twentieth century. Many are contemporary, and a majority have made their major contributions in recent years. Nearly half of them can be classified as painters; the rest are illustrators. (Such nice distinctions have had relevance for only about one-hundred years. Before that artists were artists.)

Do the working methods of our times reflect an approach different from that used by artists of earlier periods? Obviously, we don't have an exact answer. We can't drop a line to, or have a telephone interview with Rembrandt, Rubens, or Goya. However, we can look at some of their preliminary sketches, and from these deduce limited conclusions.

On the next few pages are reproduced a sampling of rough drawings by some of the great names of Western art. We cannot tell what stage of the picture development they represent. It's a good guess that most are the initial gropings for the visual statement.

What do you think? Did the artists of earlier times approach the problem of creating a picture any differently than the realistic, communicating artists of today?

The first outlines through which an able master indicates his thoughts contain the germ of anything significant that the work will offer. Raphael, Rembrandt, Poussin—I mention these particularly because they are brilliant above all through the quality of thought in their studies—make a few rapid strokes on the paper, and it seems that there is not one of them but has its importance. For intelligent eyes, the life of the work is ready to be seen everywhere; and nothing in the development of this theme, in appearance so vague, will depart in the least from the artist's conception. It has scarcely opened to the light—and already it is complete.

Eugène Delacroix

Rembrandt

Rembrandt

79

Nicholas Poussin

Giovanni Tiepolo

Peter Paul Rubens

Salvator Rosa

Francisco Goya

　　Jean Louis Forain

Robert Henri

Summing up

There is little doubt that the act of finding *ideas* and turning them into good *picture concepts* is something short of pure science. Nebulous, murky, inexact, and indistinct are the kinds of adjectives that flood the mind when reviewing the various procedures just outlined. Yet, there is a thread running through much of the material that you may find useful. Thinking the problem through and planning the picture so it will convey the message you intend are of primary importance. All else is secondary. Perhaps the methods we examined here will offer a clue that will help you uncork more promising beginnings. Awareness of the problem, patience in searching for solutions, and a little bit of luck should lead you to better, more rewarding pictures.

It is interesting to note that the sages of academe recently contrived a subject they call *cognitive psychology*—the study of how the brain assimilates knowledge. According to Dr. George Miller, a professor at Princeton University, "what the mind does best it does unconsciously . . . An act may be consciously initiated, but then the mind goes to work away from

consciousness to retrieve the necessary information. . . ."*
Apparently, scholars are only beginning to explore procedures artists have been using for centuries.

It is possible some readers will misunderstand the true value of the preliminary abstract-type sketches many artists make. Claude Croney tells about showing some of his roughs to one of his classes, suggesting they try making similar preliminary sketches. Later, looking at one man's studies, Claude asked what area of the scene he was drawing. The student replied he hadn't realized he was to select his own subject. He had simply copied Croney's sketches.

Roughs look so simplistic and meaningless it is difficult to concede their significance. In addition, their word definitions such as doodles, unconscious scribbles, and the like do little to stimulate respect. Such reaction is understandable, but it should be overcome. In the act of creating a visual concept there is some indefinable linkage between the groping of the mind for hidden ideas, the almost uncontrolled movement of the hand, and the recognition of a clue in the resultant marks by an attentive, discerning eye.

All of this may be hard to accept at face value. Possibly someday the good professors will be able to shed more light on these unfathomable processes, and all our creative fumblings will be able to function with computer-like efficiency. Until then the best way to proceed is by using the unscientific approach we have discussed. You will have to try it to find out if it works for you. My guess is you will be surprised what happens when you get the hang of it. Be sure to give the process time . . . and effort. It will take a great deal of both. Once understood you will have forged a framework on which you will be able to more easily, more surely, build better pictures.

* The New York Times, *October 12, 1982*

Composition

Merely having all the objects in your
picture that belong there and having them
well drawn is not sufficient. A man who is
dead is entirely complete in the physical
sense, and yet he is not there at all.
The same can be true with a picture.
Harvey Dunn (1884-1952)

Albin Henning *Compositional sketch*

Robert Fawcett
Sketch of a left-handed student
86

Translating concept into design

It is not possible to produce a visual concept for a picture outside the framework of a composition. Concept and composition go together as surely as bees and flowers. Each without the other is not likely to survive. Unfortunately, the mere association of a picture idea within any design arrangement does not automatically assure worthwhile results. The mind's eye concept may be breathtaking, but it must be properly translated onto the two-dimensional surface of paper, board or canvas before it can be built into a picture of merit. We will now consider how to make this happen.

The term *composition* is often used in a number of the arts. In music it signifies a harmonious sequence of notes arranged into specific forms. If you substitute *words* for notes the same definition works reasonably well for literature and poetry. In the visual arts *composition means the distribution and placement of forms, shapes, colors, and values to produce a unified and harmonious whole*. It is far easier to define and understand than it is to accomplish.

In composing a picture, a number of visual principles are helpful to recognize and apply as appropriate. These will be examined and discussed so that you will be able to use them as you convert your ideas into pictures. Keep in mind, however, that these principles are not inviolate rules to be treated as absolutes. As guidelines they can be useful, but they should not be inhibiting to what you feel is *right* for the design and purpose of your picture.

Every stage in a picture's development involves design. Sometimes this is done intuitively, often it is performed consciously. Right at the outset you are confronted with a key design problem: What picture size and proportion will best serve your concept? This is a major decision—one to be considered with care. Once the borders are established you will need to decide where to position the important forms and how large they should be. The process continues as you place more elements, suggest values, develop negative shapes, establish patterns, select and relate colors, and on and on, until it is perfect and you must find a spot to sign your name.

The search for a good composition is a constant exercise in designing. When viewed as such we all have a lot going for us. Almost everyone has an instinct and sense of design. We show it in the way we arrange furniture, or flowers, the clothes we wear, or in doodlings on the telephone book. In the crude drawings of small children there is often suggestion of strong design. The same quality is apparent in the art of many cultures. Design is a part of nature, a part of life. It consists of a relationship of a number of considerations, including shape, space, pattern, rhythm, color, texture, and balance. If there is a single key ingredient in good design it would have to do with *variety*. Let's see how all this fits together as it relates to the problems an artist faces when he starts to translate his picture idea into a composition.

Once the basic size and proportion of the picture are decided, a whole series of decisions must be made. Right at the outset, if you hope to present a realistic picture, you must determine the point of view of the scene. Next you establish the size and scale of the most important elements. In so doing you should carefully consider how the scene will be lighted and what effect the light and shadows will have on the placement of the forms. This will take experimenting and a good deal of trial and error. Usually you can accomplish this best by making a series of roughs growing out of the concept-type sketches we discussed earlier.

Slowly and with deliberation begin to refine the several variations of size, placement, and shape you feel might work. Consider the values and how the lighting will affect the established shapes. Plan, think, and question, and don't expect quick solutions.

Expression of your picture concept and answers to your design problems will be more easily managed after you understand and are familiar with some of the basics. Let's now isolate the major compositional concerns by examining some complex situations as simply and directly as possible.

Division of picture space

Pictures have been and can be designed to fit within the confines of nearly any kind of geometric shape. Squares, circles, triangles, ovals have been employed as boundaries of the picture. At times, as with some murals, separate architectural barriers must be overcome or made a part of the overall picture plan. Most often, however, we deal with the rectangle. This is the stage, the battleground for the artist's effort. Size and proportions vary greatly, but for most pictures the rectangular shape is standard. We'll start there. Assume we have established the rough dimensions of a rectangle that will serve the needs of your picture concept. In arriving at your decision, here are some factors you should consider: your mental image of the finished picture; the scale you feel will best fulfill that image; and the working size most comfortable to you in the medium you plan to use.

Because we live and operate in a three-dimensional world we are prone to *see*, within the limits of a flat surface, illusionary implications of depth and space. Such illusions are funda-

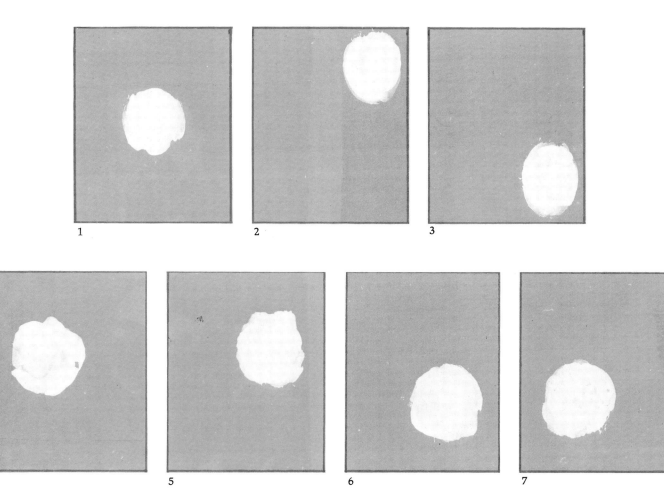

If you are working with a single major compositional element, you have these approximate placement options:

1 Place the element right in the center. Depending on the purpose and emphasis you wish to project with your picture, such placement might work well. However, the equidistant spacing to all the borders may create a monotonous effect difficult to overcome.

2 and 3 Crowding the picture's border in this manner may at times work satisfactorily, but it often generates an empty feeling in the remainder of the picture area. If such effect is undesirable, avoid this type of placement.

4, 5, 6, and 7 These locations are generally considered to be pleasing visual centers. Notice in each case the division of space to the borders is uneven. This helps create visual interest and variety.

mental to the process of creating a believable picture. Scale and size relationships of elements within the picture, overlapping and use of values and color are crucial to this process. All of this must be considered in the formation of even the simplest composition.

Rembrandt   The Metropolitan Museum of Art, New York   **Oskar Kokoschka**   The Museum of Modern Art, New York

If we were to create a picture with but a single major element in it, such as some portraits, we could place that element anywhere in the picture space and be assured it would garner the viewer's attention. As the obvious area of interest it would automatically attract visual attention. By experimenting we could quickly discover a number of pleasing ways to place the lone element in the picture space. Some of these trial-and-error positions undoubtedly would have more appeal than others. It would be a simple matter to select the seemingly most satisfying placement and, *voilà,* our one element compositional problem is solved.

Be assured such compositions usually become more complex because of background considerations, color, pattern, values, and so on, but in essence the placement choices remain relatively simple.

Pablo Picasso   The Metropolitan Museum of Art, New York

Thomas Eakins   The Phillips Gallery, Washington, D.C.

Placement and linear divisions

Successful pictures do not necessarily depend on specific linear divisions of space as a basis for their compositions. A number of painters, including Kandinsky, Klee, Matisse, Davis, and Picasso, to mention a few, often relied on a scattered, overall design. Nor is this approach limited to the modern idiom. Old masters such as Bosch and Bruegel also employed this schema. However, it is more common to divide the rectangular picture area horizontally, vertically, diagonally, or in some combination of two or more, as diagrammed on the opposite page. There are, of course, innumerable variations and modifications applicable to each dominant theme.

Such linear picture planning may seem overly simplistic, yet it is a logical outgrowth of what we observe in the real world. Every unobstructed view we encounter on land or sea offers comparable divisions between sections of earth, water, and sky. Realistic interpretations incorporating these vistas inevitably require recognition of such spatial breakup. We are also surrounded with multiple space divisions when we move indoors. Few interiors are devoid of floors, walls, ceilings, doors, et cetera, all of which establish boundaries of intersecting planes. We see these intersections as definite vertical, horizontal, and—often because of perspective—diagonal lines. The universality of space divisions, be they natural or manmade, make them dominant design factors.

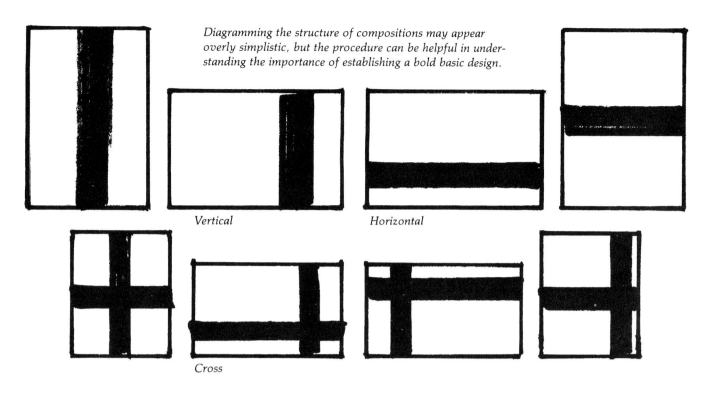

Diagramming the structure of compositions may appear overly simplistic, but the procedure can be helpful in understanding the importance of establishing a bold basic design.

Vertical

Horizontal

Cross

Diagonal

Centered

Combination

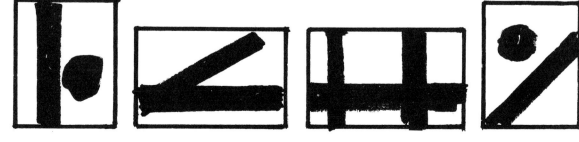

The square and other formats

The form and function of certain shapes have fascinated people since the dawn of time. The circle, square, and pyramid have long been held in special, even mystical esteem. Logically, artists often use these structures as the basis for their compositions. Many probably feel such a format is more organized and controllable than the simpler space divisions diagrammed on page 93. Nor is the approach particularly restricting, as there are many modifications of the primary basic forms. These include the ellipse, the figure 8 and the *S* curve, all of which are cousins of the circle. Also available is the triangle in many configurations, as well as its derivatives, the diagonal and the *L* shape. All are offshoots of the square or pyramid. The manner in which these devices are sometimes employed will be pointed out in the captions of appropriate illustrations.

Of all the compositional structures used by artists throughout the ages, perhaps the most common is the square. Although frequently modified from its geometric symmetry, a discernible square shape within the confines of a rectangular picture can serve to rivet attention with a wonderful force. The square can be used in numerous ways, as the accompanying examples demonstrate. Many Renaissance painters worked within such formats, particularly when their compositions contained prominent architectural elements. As with the bull's eye of a circle, the viewer's attention is attracted towards the center of a square. Thus an object placed near this vicinity is given extra emphasis. If such an area is combined with strong value contrast and given color or textural intensity, a compelling interest center is created.

To center or not to center

Linear placement in any form can be a bugaboo even for the experienced artist if rules are rigidly followed. The positioning of an element in a composition is a relative thing. Its effectiveness will be enhanced or diminished by how the values, edges, color, pattern, textures, and lines are used throughout the picture.

Many teachers warn students against placing important elements in the center of the picture space. To do so, they say, will create equal areas in the composition that will be static

Masaccio, *The Tribute Money (detail)*

Brancaoci Chapel, Sta Mario del Carmine, Florence

Here is an interesting example of the use of a rectangle within a rectangle. With minimal architectural definition, a contained square shape is established at the right, isolating Saint Peter and the Roman tax collector. Near the center is the hand of Saint Peter making the money payment. The other figures are grouped so as not to detract from the telling action at the right.

The artist, considered to be a forerunner of Michelangelo, painted this fresco shortly before his death. What might this man have accomplished if he had lived beyond his twenty-seventh year.

Maxfield Parrish, *Jack Sprat*

This painting was an advertisement for Swift's ham. Notice how the product occupies the exact center of the well-planned square-within-a-rectangular picture space. Parrish must have been fond of this type of arrangement, for he used it in many of his compositions.

and uninteresting. It is well to be aware of this possibility. However, to treat such advice as an absolute prohibition is to deny the worth of a great number of excellent paintings from da Vinci to Wyeth that are based on center placement. As forthcoming examples will testify, the problems attendant to center placement can usually be overcome with intelligent use of values, color, and pattern.

The fine American painter, Doris Lee, replied when asked about her theory of compositional placement, "I decide what's important and I place it in the middle." Perhaps Doris was speaking frivolously, but her paintings suggest she frequently follows such a plan, usually with splendid results.

Linear placement of the elements deserves careful attention in organizing your composition, but you are well-advised to avoid rigid rules. With an open mind and a little research you'll discover that every maxim you ever heard about composition can be strongly refuted by some of the world's most renowned paintings. Let the rules serve as guides and warnings of possible difficulties, but don't become a slave to them.

Formulas for compositions

"The unity of a work of art," said Aristotle in the third century B.C., should be such that "if any of the parts be either transposed or taken way, the whole will be destroyed or changed." In the ensuing millenniums a vast array of artists have done their best to satisfy the great philosopher's dictum. Understandably, few could claim success. As anyone who has ever tried knows, organizing all compositional elements into a faultless relationship can be as bewildering as the theory of relativity.

Considering the complexity and frustration of this puzzle, it is small wonder a number of artists have devoted much time in searching for the Holy Grail of design—a formula to determine perfect picture placement. Throughout the history of Western art several intriguing ideas have surfaced, usually in the form of mathematical ratios. One of the most prevailing is a geometric proportion referred to as the *golden mean* or *golden section*.

The theorem was formulated by another Greek sage, Euclid, who postulated, "A straight line is said to have been cut in extreme and mean ratio when, as the whole line is to the greater segment, so is the greater to the less." This unique proportion may be more easily understood by studying the marginal comments and diagrams. Advocates claim the golden section is aesthetically superior to all other proportions. Possibly—if you believe it requires *precise* unity within variation to please the eye. Such a premise is difficult to verify.

Several outstanding artists are said to have based major compositions on this theory. *The Surrender of Breda* (on page 97) is purported to be an example, although an analysis of the

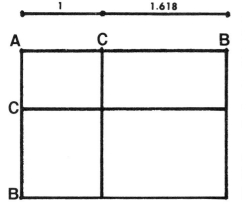

The golden mean is called the perfect proportion. The relationship of 1 to 1.618 can be repeated over and over in each subdivided rectangle maintaining the ratio:
   AC is to CB as CB is to AB.
Placing your major picture elements at these intersections some think will assure a superior composition.

Velazquez, *Surrender of Breda*

work shows enough deviation to make this apppear dubious. In any case, it defies credibility, as well as Aristotle, to imagine minor adjustments in placement would seriously jeopardize the picture's masterpiece status. In truth, the approximate space divisions achievable with the golden mean are evident in many forms and designs, the creations of which were unhindered by methodical measurement. It seems ludicrous to conclude perfection is possible only through calculated construction. By its nature art is more in tune with intuition than with science.

Many artists and teachers who support the conscientious application of the perfect placement principle maintain the geometric formula was frequently employed by many famous

Leonardo da Vinci ▮ *Mona Lisa*

Michelangelo ▮

98

artists. Perhaps, but the evidence is evasive. Who, where, and how many used it? With piqued interest I resolved to conduct a small, admittedly unscientific survey, and plot the golden mean for every noted picture I came across. Over a period of months I randomly measured and recorded hundreds of reproductions of great paintings. The easiest way to locate the golden section is to multiply each picture dimension by 0.62; or if you prefer, divide each side by 1.6. Either way will locate the division point for the composition's height and width. The intersection of the horizontal and vertical lines drawn between the opposing equal measures will establish the *ideal* spot to place an important element and the center of interest.

Of all the pictures examined the number apparently based on the perfect ratio was extremely small—smaller than suggested by the digest of the survey illustrated on these pages.

To avoid controversy, only portraits are shown as examples on the premise that the eyes, or, at least, the center portion of the face represents an unchallengeable center of interest. With but one exception all of the pictures used here are self-portraits. This was done only from an interest point of view. If other subjects and types of paintings were exhibited there would be no appreciable difference in the percentage of pictures apparently employing the golden mean.

A glance at the examples reveals but one painting to be in exact accord with the perfect measurements. Strangely, this sole conforming work is by an artist you would not suspect of being overly concerned with the niceties of mathematical placement. It is the picture by Van Gogh called, *Self-Portrait With Cut Ear.* The painting was made shortly after the artist had attacked his colleague, Gauguin, with a razor. Then he cut off a portion of his own ear and presented it to a lady friend as a gift. It is difficult to make a strong case for Vincent's analytical state of mind at the time.

You'll notice that in most of the examples the eyes of the subject are located close to the ideal spot, a few are very close, while some, including the prestigious *Mona Lisa*, miss the mark by a wide margin.

It could be argued that the picture's center of interest need only be placed in the general proximity of the golden section. Such reasoning seems to invalidate the purpose of the principle. Why use the formula at all? Why not follow your intuitive sense of design all the way? Indeed, that appears to be the best approach. Certainly it is the way the majority of artists work. One thing is sure: The excellence of a work of art is not diminished if the focal center fails to coincide exactly with the coordinates of the golden mean.

The intent here is not to discredit or put down the celebrated ratio. It may have some value if treated in general terms. It can serve as a starting point, a helpful rule of thumb, if you are in doubt about the positioning of a pivotal form.

The intersection of the horizontal and vertical lines drawn to the opposing marks will place the golden section of each picture.

Fantin-Latour

National Academy of Design

Eakins

Uffizi, Florence

Art Institute of Chicago

Degas

Corot
National Gallery, London

Van Gogh

Gemeentemuseum, The Hague

Mondrian

Cézanne

Metropolitan Museum of Art

El Greco

Raphael   Uffizi, Florence

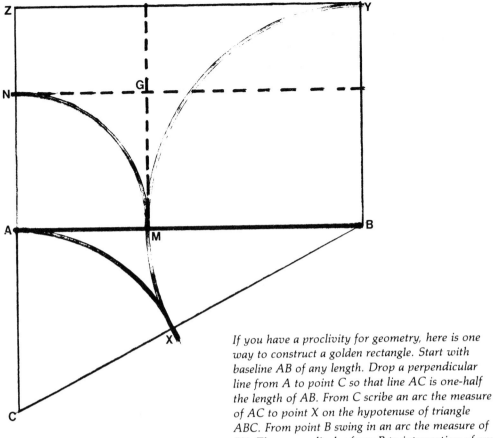

If you have a proclivity for geometry, here is one way to construct a golden rectangle. Start with baseline AB of any length. Drop a perpendicular line from A to point C so that line AC is one-half the length of AB. From C scribe an arc the measure of AC to point X on the hypotenuse of triangle ABC. From point B swing in an arc the measure of BX. The perpendicular from B to intersection of arc at Y is the height of the desired rectangle. Complete rectangle ABYZ. Point M on line AB establishes the golden ratio. An arc from A, the length of AM, will place N. M and N are the coordinates for the golden section at G.

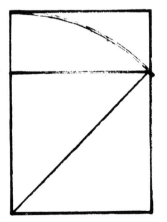

Dynamic symmetry is based on the so-called root-2 projection. This is created by extending a square according to the arc of the square's diagonal, as diagrammed above. In the 1920's this system was as talked about as the Charleston. Now it is little more than a curiosity.

Over the years several other *scientific* approaches to design and composition have acquired a handful of loyal devotees. These include *dynamic symmetry, grids,* and most recently in graphic design and architecture, the *modular* system. All of these procedures have a kinship with the golden mean. Their purpose, adherents claim, is to free the artist from the time-consuming burden of trial-and-error decision making or faulty inspirational selections. The majority of these, at times brain-boggling analyses, are games best left to the machinations of would-be mathematicians. In general they offer little of value to the painter. A few artistic giants such as El Greco may have occasionally composed pictures with the golden section or other projections in mind, but it is a fair bet they would have jettisoned the exercise in mid-passage if the results ran counter to the dictates of their visual instincts.

The perfect placement formula to solve all compositional problems is a tantalizing notion, but like the Fountain of Youth, there is scant evidence such things can or should exist.

Fra Angelico   *The Vatican*

Cross

Examples of space division

The next few pages show examples of work by a wide variety
of artists. The basic compositional structure of each picture is
identified. An infinite number of variations are available
when using combinations of the basic space divisions. However, in many cases the simple straightforward structure
works best. Elemental design speaks more powerfully than
the cluttered and contrived.

It may be of interest to note that in at least two of the eleven
examples, from pages 101 to 107, the placement of the center
of interest is close to the mathematical measurements of the
golden mean. The placement is so close it seems fair to conclude that these artists based their compositions on the formula. Whether they did it consciously or by chance is not
known. Can you identify the paintings? The answers are giv-
en in the footnote on page 107.

Center

Leonardo da Vinci

Vertical

Pablo Picasso, *The Woman of Majorca*

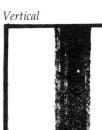

Andrew Wyeth, *April Wind*

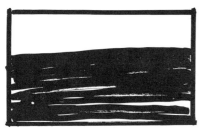

Horizontal

Joaquin Sorolla, *Sketch of Columbus*

Cross

Frans Hals, *Malle Babbe*   *The Metropolitan Museum of Art, New York*

Centered

Edouard Manet, *Bar at Folies-Bergère*

Combination

*Notice the use of the tent poles
to contain the interest area.*

Combination

John Steuart Curry
The Flying Codonas

Edward Hopper

These preliminary sketches clearly indicate the kind of space division the artist had in mind as he developed the painting shown below. Hopper often used interiors and buildings as the dominant elements in his pictures. Many of his compositions are keyed to the effectiveness of a square within a rectangle. Here a triangular format is obvious.

Sketches through the courtesy of the Whitney Museum of American Art, New York.

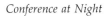

Conference at Night

The Wichita Art Museum, the Roland P. Murdock Collection

Winslow Homer

Museum of Fine Arts, Boston

Multiple objects in the picture

Diagramming and explaining basic compositional functions in simple abstract or geometric terms seems overly elemental. The process begs the issue because we rarely encounter picture problems isolated in such a controlled environment. However, to be sure we are homing on the same wavelength these few examples are offered.

Developing pictures, even portraits that concentrate on one major element, usually requires dealing with several objects in the composition. When two or more important elements are involved the number of size and placement options begins to multiply. Wherever you place the elements things begin to happen. Selecting the most appropriate solution requires thought and care.

If the several objects are made to be similar in size and spaced fairly evenly, the result is likely to be a scattered look. If this is the effect you wish, and at times it may be, such placement might be desirable. If it is not what you had in mind you should find some other solution. You can choose from a variety of possibilities. Besides altering the sizes, you can overlap one or more of the forms or crop some areas at one or more of the borders. Also, the values and color you use will play an influential role.

The compositions apparently based on the golden mean are by Leonardo da Vinci (102) and Frans Hals (104). An argument could be made to include the Winslow Homer painting shown above. It depends on whether the bell or the man is identified as the center of interest. If you consider the bell the dominant element, which, indeed, it appears to be in color, then this picture is also close to the ideal proportional placement.

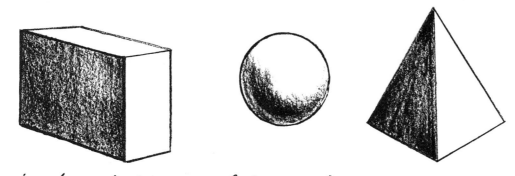

Using these basic forms let's see what problems we run into when we start to arrange them within the picture space.

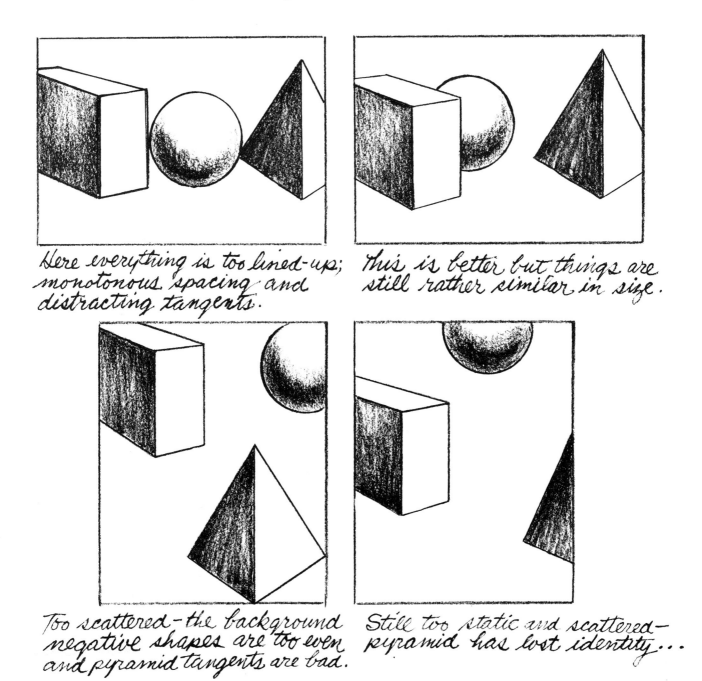

Here everything is too lined-up; monotonous spacing and distracting tangents.

This is better but things are still rather similar in size.

Too scattered - the background negative shapes are too even and pyramid tangents are bad.

Still too static and scattered - pyramid has lost identity...

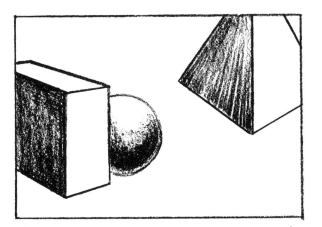

Negative path through center is not good; also eye-trap at corner.

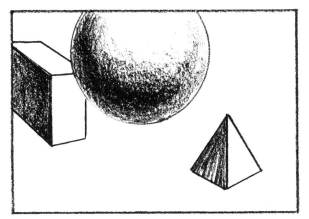

Forms read clearly, but negative areas seem too important.

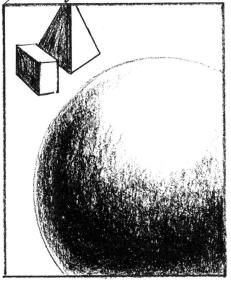

Sphere and cube appear lost and crowded in corner...

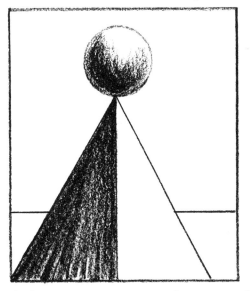

This looks contrived but it might work as a design.

Cluttered, uninteresting placement and smaller forms too even in size.

Box and sphere too evenly spaced, and the pyramid has lost its identity.

Using the picture space

A wide range of possibilities is open for consideration when approaching every composition. Some are so obvious they seem not worth exploring. However, as with the search for picture ideas, compositions are evolutionary. A hasty conclusion based on a preconceived idea may prove satisfactory, but chances are against it. Without some experimenting your picture plan may fall short of the exciting twist and eye-stopper you would really like. You'll never be sure you are starting down the right road unless you take the time to explore the options open to you.

A first and major concern is to decide what you want to emphasize. On the opposite page is a simple example dealing with a single subject. Nothing complex here, but still decisions must be made as to what is important and how best to show it. Any of the sketches might work; it all depends on your concept. If you had in mind to suggest a lonely pup, the initial rough might serve well. On the other hand, if you hope to show more of his personality the last sketch might have more appeal. The range of view from distant to close-up and any stage in between is a factor you should consider for every picture you undertake.

On the following pages are some roughs showing a variety of picture possibilities dealing with a limited number of elements. This time we will work with simplified but realistic forms. All the compositions have the same cast of characters: a horse and rider, a desert type tree, a landmass with a mesa/butte, and the sky. By changing the viewpoint, the scale of the elements, and the relationships between them and the picture area, overlapping and cropping, an almost limitless number of solutions become available. Some solutions will work better than others. Which one is best? That depends on your concept and what it is you want to express.

Bear in mind there are no right or wrong solutions to placement problems. There are no hard and fast rules to follow. What does not work well for one picture concept may be the perfect solution for another. Learning to be aware of potential trouble spots, however, is essential. Often difficulties are easy to overcome once you recognize their existence.

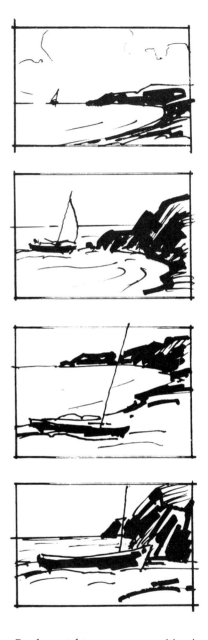

Fundamental to every composition is the decision dealing with how close you want the subject. Would it be best to keep the boat in the distance, allowing more emphasis on the scenery? Or would it be better to show a closer view? It all depends on what you decide is important.

111

How can we use these elements in the picture space?

Lets try having the horse and rider in the distance ...

Or closer with more butte ...

Should the tree be bigger and the rocks smaller?

Or even larger with the rider closer?

How about a vertical?

With the horse and rider closer...

Even closer? Still closer—whoops, we've lost the horse...

The horse is gone but maybe we don't need him.

Now we've gone this far, why not even closer?

Perhaps it would be better to back off and look down on the scene...

Or, look up at it?

The possibilities are endless. What would you do?

Depth—overlapping and cropping

Flat space within the confines of a rectangle is not a part of the world's normal condition. Instinctively we perceive space as having depth. Visually the natural space formations we see and understand—earth and everything upon it, sky, water—all have depth. Space lacking depth is unreal. All our observation confirms these basic facts: The sky is bright and seemingly limitless; the earth is dense with color and textural gradients ranging from light and coarse when close at hand, to diffused and fine in the distance; water is reflective, deep, or shallow, and of transitory character. Conditioned as we are to our physical environment we readily translate any visual clue shown on a flat surface to a perceptual equivalent in three dimensions. The artist makes use of all these percepts in establishing the illusion of space and depth on the flat surface that is his drawing or painting.

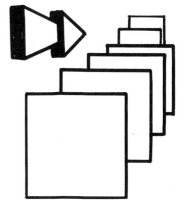

One of the obvious ways to show depth is by overlapping elements in a picture. Visually, even with the overlapping of flat planes of the same size, the eye tends to accept a condition of depth. When overlapping and diminution of size is combined a stronger suggestion of space is created. The act of overlapping one form immediately involves cropping another. The two procedures must work together.

Overlapping and cropping forms within a picture must be done with deliberation. A number of things can go wrong and generate disturbing conditions. Things to watch for include undesirable tangents, a form's loss of identity, the creation of uninteresting or distracting shapes, development of unwanted directional emphasis, and more. The examples on the following pages explore some of the aspects of overlapping and cropping. All such problems can and do occur in almost every composition. Let's look at some.

To start we'll use these basic forms to diagram some observations about placement. All these problems can occur when several elements are brought together in a picture space.

Why not place them just as they might appear on a shelf? This is _not_ too good because...

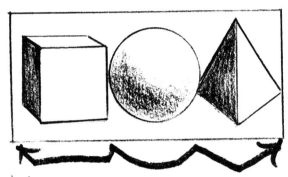

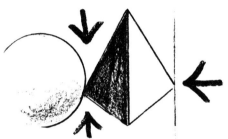

The negative shapes — the spaces around the forms — are much too even and consistent

The line created by the base of the forms is uninteresting and each form bumping the next rivets attention at tangent areas.

Eye-traps such as this call attention to unimportant areas.

Now the overlapping is good and the shape line is more interesting, but there is still a difficult tangent and eye-trap.

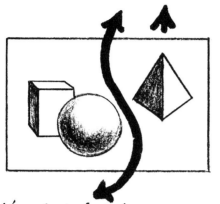

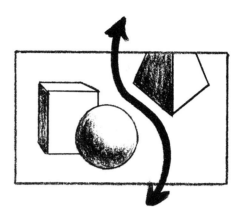

Not bad, but in overcoming one problem we've created another. Now there is too much emphasis leading up and out of the picture.

This helps but there is still a compelling negative path through the picture.

How about a vertical shape? Here things are too much in line and the sphere and cube have lost identity.

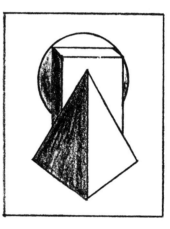

Still crowded, but the shapes are clearer... how would it work as a horizontal?

Better negative shapes, but alignment is dull...

Many forms are easily recognizable when only a small portion of the whole is visible. In a suitable environment common objects such as a chair can be cropped radically without loss of identity. The segment you show in your picture may be small, but it should be significant in shape and positioning.

Identity of forms

Visually we know things according to their shapes, size, color, and texture. If any of these properties are missing, or present in unexpected proportion, we are likely to question the object's identity, or label it as counterfeit. Of all the conditions necessary for quick identification, *shape* is of particular significance. If the shape is not clear it is hard to recognize. Paradoxically, most things can be readily identified if but a tiny portion is visible. In truth, much of what we see is in some kind of fragmented form. Our line of vision is forever blocked by something in the way of what we are looking at. Few objects in everyday life reside on pedestals allowing unobstructed scrutiny. The person we see outside the window is partially hidden by the curtain, the mullions, a portion of the house and the limb of a tree. Things are not much better indoors. The clock on the table is almost invisible because of the books and potted plant in front of it. Overlapping, cropping, and the consequent fragmentation of things we see are so common we seldom give the matter a second thought.

Not so for the artist if he is concerned with projecting some kind of realism in his picture. The limited universe of the picture space places special restrictions on everything exhibited. The audience studying the composition cannot search out a better vantage point, or shift an obstructing object for needed clarification. The artist in his omnipotence freezes the placement of the picture elements as inexorably as hardened concrete. What the viewer sees is what there is. Nothing more is available.

How the artist manages this burden and solves this problem is in part what separates him from the photographer. The camera cannot discriminate in what is shown. The artist can and must. He selects and arranges each element so it will work in the composition exactly as he wants it to. Any overlapped and cropped form should not be so mutilated as to suffer loss of identity. In representational pictures, unidentifiable elements should be considered for alteration or elimination. This does not mean every part of a realistic picture must be boiled-out and made specific. Indeed, not. Vagueness and lack of definition can incite appeal. A viewer armed with sufficient visual clues is usually ready to conjure his own recognizable image. What causes trouble are those elements in a picture that are rendered with some definition, but fall short when it comes to purpose and identity because of their placement.

Determining how a form can be cropped and not lose its

identity is best accomplished through experimentation. Certain common objects in a predictable environment can undergo severe cropping without loss of identity. The familiar type chair, as illustrated, clearly shows it can be reduced to a small segment and remain meaningful if incorporated in a scene where you would expect such furniture to exist. If one of the small portions was used, say, in a landscape, it would probably appear as a distracting, incongruous shape. Less familiar objects, such as the old ship's lantern, need be more judiciously handled or their purpose and function will be meaningless to the viewer.

Whenever figures are included in a composition, special care in cropping is advisable. Not only must the positioning work in the overall design, but critical areas such as the head and face often require careful adjustments to achieve the desired impact. (See Fawcett illustrations on page123.) In general, it is wise to avoid extensive cropping at major anatomical joints if you hope to keep the figure from looking deformed or dismembered. You should also keep your figures from appearing to bump or rest on the picture borders. When figure cropping is required, do so with deliberation, but do it decisively.

Less familiar objects such as this old ship's lantern must be cropped with care or their function and purpose may be unclear or misunderstood by the viewer.

Clarity of shapes

Even the most familiar objects, when seen in poor lighting or at unusual angles, can be difficult to identify. Often the carefully selected silhouettes of the form will be the angle most easily recognized, as is the case with these ducks. In the straight-on front view the birds are difficult to identify, but in profile a bird-watcher would be able to tell you that the floating duck, above right, is a red-breasted merganser, and the one below is a mallard.

Confusion of shapes, as demonstrated here, can cause trouble. Parts of some shapes are clear enough, but what is happening overall is not immediately apparent, either in the diagram or the sketch. Sometimes adjustments of values and color will overcome these problems. The point is to recognize the difficulty so that it can be modified. Often a relatively small change in positioning will make things clear. In this case, slight revisions are not sufficient to solve the shape problem. Radical change in positioning seems necessary.

George Bellows, *The Big Dory*

This colorful composition by an outstanding artist has much merit. However, on close look the figures pushing the boat create several areas of confusion. What is the white shape growing out of the center sailor's head that makes him look like a rakish unicorn? Perhaps it is distant surf breaking against the big rock, or is it a reefed jib on the small sailboat? In any case, it is not explained and as a result becomes an unnecessary point of attraction that does the picture no good. In a similar way, the spit of rocks leading into the sea seems to grow out of the shoulders of the men at the right. These background boulders are so closely related to the men in size, shape, color, value, and position that they appear to be another unexplained arm. Small adjustments in both areas would make for greater clarity and rid the scene of confusion.

In our times, a scene with oxen plowing a field is not common enough for the viewer to understand what is going on unless all the important shapes are clearly visible. Here it was necessary to turn the forms to approximately this position before the shapes would read at a glance.

121

Robert Fawcett

This delightful vignette owes much of its feeling of depth and unity to careful overlapping. Notice the hat, the umbrella, the position of the man's feet, the way his knee overlaps the tea table, and on and on until your view is stopped by the framed portrait that directs your gaze back to the woman in the winged chair. It is a simple, but well-organized illustration.

Robert Fawcett

Here is another fine example by the master draftsman. One of the requisites for this illustration was to accurately represent an eighteenth-century print shop. The artist became so involved with the details and the equipment that he found, at this late planning stage, the head of the important master printer was almost completely blocked by the foreground pressman's extended arms. Bob frequently worked from photographs of posed models, and such unfortunate juxtaposition is a common occurrence in the camera's product. It was a relatively simple problem to correct; Fawcett merely added about six inches to the old printer's height. The result is shown in the small pullout from a succeeding preliminary drawing and the nearly completed rendering at the right.

Tangents

Tangents, where lines or forms just touch but do not decisively intersect, can appreciably affect a composition. Once you become aware of tangents in compositions you will discover they occur with amazing frequency. They are not always bad; in fact, at times they can add just the right degree of emphasis to a given area. Often, however, they are an unexpected surprise and must be dealt with. One thing is certain: They seem to be attracted to key areas the way magnets are to iron. Fortunately, small adjustments in placement or value will usually take care of the difficulty.

Logically, you should be able to spot troublesome tangent areas at the preliminary sketch stage and make the necessary modifications without undue concern. But most sketches are just that, sketchy—rough approximations of what you plan to do. Things begin to happen when refinements of value, shapes, textures, and color are added. It is easy to become involved with details of rendering and fail to notice a tangent that compositionally is as obvious as a wart on the end of your neighbor's nose. The small sketch of the sailboat at the top of the page is a case in point.

Notice how the bow collides with the distant landmass. Slightly shifting either the boat or the land would allow the vessel to generate an illusion of greater speed and movement—an important consideration for any realistic painting of a vessel under sail.

The small sketches at the left suggest two ways the land problem could be solved. The hull is lowered somewhat in relation to the land in one sketch. The other shows the effect if the land were brought closer. This has the advantage of giving stronger contrasting background for the sails.

Other possible solutions would be to lighten the values of the land and leave the positioning pretty much alone; the land could be reduced in value and size, or it could be eliminated altogether.

One way or another, corrections must be made. Otherwise, everytime you look at the picture all you'll see is that terrible tangent.

This is the type of scene that delights the soul of many on-the-spot sketchers—a large mass of rocks, the sea, and an old beached boat. With good weather, and a full paint box, what more could you want?

You wouldn't think you would encounter tangent trouble here, but you can bet your favorite brush you will. Look at the lineup of the boat's transom and the base of the rocks. Unless you are on the lookout for such a situation it is likely to find its way into your picture as shown in the top rough sketch.

Once noted, the solution is fairly easy . . . just reposition the boat slightly so that the stern is visually clear of the rocks, or move it back a bit to create positive overlap.

Directional lines

Lines, as such, do not exist in nature. Visually they come into being as the division between forms, colors and values. Possibly because of their amorphous nature, people are always fascinated by them.

Did you ever consider the pervasive metaphorical addiction we all have to the word *line?* It is doubtful we could communicate without it. From life *line* to the top of the *line,* and thence to the bottom *line,* this four-letter word is a part of everyone's lexicon. We walk a *line,* follow a *line,* ride a bus *line* to the air *line,* finally reaching our destination via the rail *lines.* In the meantime, we read the *lines,* and between the *lines,* question the party *line,* while we plan a new tag *line.* We respect West Point's long gray *line,* not to mention the chorus *line.* While our football team holds the *line,* there is someone on the other end of the telephone *line* giving us a *line.* Finally we reach the bitter end—the end of the *line.*

Small wonder artists become engrossed with lines when creating pictures they hope will communicate to others. We all think in terms of lines, and it is part of the human condition to line things up. When we see a line or semblance of one we sight down it like the barrel of a rifle to see where it leads. For these reasons one of the more obvious compositional ploys is what is generally referred to as *directional lines.*

Depending on the picture's subject, these may take form within the composition as actual lines, such as painted stripes on a highway, or just the edges of the road itself as it cuts its swath through the land. (See the Briggs sketch on the opposite page.) Nor must lines be as conspicuous as railroad tracks leading off to a distant horizon. The shapes of buildings, a series of windows, doors, or other architectural features when observed in perspective generate noticeable lines our eyes follow like an obedient bird dog. These elements are evident in the Corot painting on page 127.

Many other things, such as the limbs of trees, fence posts, utility poles, as well as the edges of almost everything from barges, buses, and billboards to people, if composed in the right configuration, can create strong visual emphasis to direct our attention to a particular place. In the real, hodgepodge world we need signs to tell us which way to go. A well-composed picture needs no such accouterments. If you know what you are doing you can use most of your picture elements to beckon unsuspecting observers directly to the center of interest without any delay or distracting detours. If you properly organize the picture, the viewers will never get lost. In fact, as long as the picture holds their attention, even though their eyes may stray from the focal center, all avenues of sight will constantly redirect their attention back to the chosen spot.

The astute observer might point out that often the directional lines we are discussing could as logically lead the view-

Jean-Baptiste Corot

Austin Briggs

er's attention *away* from the desired compositional area as effectively as they lead us to the center of interest. True, lines are not always one-way streets, but picture borders usually make them function that way. By the nature of how we look at things, we are attracted inward, towards the middle of a universe, rather than outward, to the more vague surroundings.

Another facet of mortal makeup useful to the artist is our propensity to know what someone else is looking at. Did you ever see someone on a crowded sidewalk staring skyward, and not steal an upward glance yourself to see what the person was looking at? If you are free of such instinctive herd habits you may consider yourself exceptional. Most of us are compelled to know what the other guy finds so interesting. This fixation carries over when we look at pictures. It is a useful device for the artist. He knows the observer's attention will follow the course of the gaze held by the picture's principal players. As certain as sin, we'll take a bead on the line of sight of the person or animal illustrated to discover what is holding their attention.

The best way to see directional lines and other compositional considerations is to analyze a variety of pictures. On the following pages a number of examples are examined with this in mind. These reproductions are all in black and white. Bear in mind, color can play a key role in the final effectiveness of a composition, and in some instances it may overcome difficulties or deficiencies not evident when the picture is reduced to a scale of gray.

Critical advice

In assuming the role of the critic, a word of caution is in order. When we appraise the works created in periods other than our own, it is wise to remind ourselves that the notion of beauty is fickle and easily confused with style. Like fashions, the pictures we extol today may retain some lasting merit, but the test of time will surely relegate many to justified obscurity. If future generations recall the art of our day they will probably do so with the kind of amused tolerance we reserve for yesteryear's costumes.

Art is evolutionary. Quality does not change, but the means of expression does. The concept, procedures, and purpose of a picture are influenced by the state of values held by the artist at the time of the picture's inception. The temper and expectations of the audience for which the work was intended must also be noted. Relatively few pictures past or present, are created solely to satisfy the aesthetic urges of the artist. The standards we use to judge the work of the past should take into consideration, as much as possible, the reigning criteria of that day. Humbly we can hope coming generations will afford our offerings equal charity and forbearance.

Robert Fawcett

This preliminary sketch demonstrates you don't need roads, railroad tracks, or architecture to use directional lines effectively. This simple arrangement of overlapping figures forcefully directs our attention to the hand holding the pencil. The poses of the men, the positioning of the arms and hands, the folds of the drapery, the curve of the paper, and the angle of their glance, all rivet the emphasis on the one key area.

Jan van Eyck, *Adoration of the Madonna*

The van Eyck brothers lived in the fifteenth century. In addition to being among the first to work in oil, they are credited as the forerunners of realistic genre painting. Technically, as evidenced here, Jan had a masterful control of the medium and a remarkable feeling for light and textures. The van Eycks' contribution to the revolution in church art cannot be minimized. However, this composition remains a stiff, formal representation of symbols. The figures show little relationship to each other. Individually each section is beautifully rendered, but taken as a whole the picture lacks unity and concentration of emphasis. It is, in reality, three pictures.

Because of their center placement within the structural square, reinforced by the perspective lines of the floor, rug, and architecture, the Madonna and child are a strong interest area. The other figures supply no support to the central theme. Each one is looking in a different direction with apparent disregard for the rest of the group. Did the artist wish to express a dichotomy of interest by freezing individual portraits in a symbolic design to please his patrons? Possibly. But it is more likely, because of his time and influences, he did not understand one unified pictorial statement can be more effective than three that are isolated and unrelated.

Pieter Bruegel, *Hunters in the Snow*

Ranked as one of the greatest landscapes of all time, this sixteenth century painting is a masterfully organized composition. Here is the essence of variety within unity. Notice the way the grouping of the hunters and hounds in the foreground becomes part of the cadence of the line-up of trees leading down the hill. The eye is constantly led to the pond with the skaters in the middle distance. From there you look up at the mountains which, in turn, direct you to the soaring bird and the tree limbs, and back to the men and hounds. Visually it is an oval path from which it is difficult to escape. If your gaze happens to seek an exit along the frozen stream at the lower right, your interest is held by two small figures strategically placed on the ice to redirect your line of sight up the crest of the hill to the roofs and back to the pond. Everywhere you look you find isolated spots of interest; but inexorably you are drawn back to the focal center.

Gustave Courbet, *The Forest*

Color, values and texture have much to do with the appeal of this painting, but in this black and white reproduction we can easily identify the artist's effective use of directional lines. The focal area in the center of the composition is but a slight modification on the theme of the square we have already discussed.

Camille Pissarro *The Pork Butcher*

Honoré Daumier, *Don Quixote and Sancho Panza*

Daumier was noted for his use of strong, dominant shapes, as demonstrated in this picture. With a minimum of detail, his work generates mood and authority based on shape and values. No diagrams are needed to pin down the center of interest here. Notice in particular the careful positioning of the horse and rider as they race to the left. If their silhouette were not minimized by the background hill, the composition would have two competing areas of interest and suffer because of it. Powerful statements require bold simplicity.

← *Pissarro was one of the best of the Impressionists. Unlike a number of his colleagues, he seldom sacrificed compositional considerations in a headlong quest for color effects. In this case, the foreground figure's head is intriguingly established as the center of interest by the positioning of the canopy supports. The viewer's attention is trapped in a series of squares as effectively as the Fra Angelico painting on page 101. As the eye travels to the left along the horizontal bar, it is turned back by the angle of the head of the woman at the left margin. Her gaze leads us over to the woman at the right. Her eyes force us to look down at the table which, in turn, takes us back to the main figure.*

133

Alfred Sisley

The forceful directional lines of the bridge visually take the observer across the river to the white building on the opposite shore. Since there is not much to hold your attention in this vicinity, your eye either slips down the roadway to the right and out of the picture, or you are attracted to the activity in the shadows under the bridge. Here, instead of excitement, you find confusion and don't know where to look. What success this painting has depends on color. When strong directional lines are incorporated in a picture they should lead to some area of interest. This obviously was recorded as a "slice of nature." To make an effective painting the composition needs better organization.

This sketch is based on a watercolor by Winslow Homer. Only the placement is meant to be faithful to the painting. It is included here to make the point that even knowledgeable artists sometimes fall short when it comes to important compositional considerations.

As an experienced observer of the sea, Homer knew the size and proportions of ocean waves. He frequently chose to suggest the limited vision one has when close to the swell's surface. At times, as in this instance where he carried his sense of reality to such an extreme, identity of the forms is obscured, and the observer is hard put to know what is going on. Showing a little more of the dory would have made a more understandable picture.

Critics have condemned the Yankee painter because of his illustrator heritage and approach. In this composition, the difficulty rests in faulty illustration more than with the painting.

Lynn Bogue Hunt

These ducks are grouped into a beautifully controlled center design. The angles of the bodies, wings, and pointing bills all direct attention to the lower right. Here our eye meets a finger of land that swiftly leads to the left and the tip of the lower duck's wing. This takes us right back in a circular path to the focal center. The spiked grass in the foreground and the distant hills echo this circular eye passage.

135

Edgar Degas

Compositionally Degas did some outlandish things—and almost always they worked. One of the reasons his pictures are so exciting is that he seldom settled for the obvious.

In this painting notice all the things a prudent artist wouldn't do: strong directional lines leading out of the picture; obvious tangents (see circled section of diagram); mutilation-type cropping of the foot at the right; and both figures looking out of the picture in opposite directions. Yet the composition doesn't fall apart. Why?

The overlapping unity of shape, color, and value of the dancers' skirts holds them together, each on one leg. The value contrasts in the tangent area of the arms create an area of interest more forceful than the heads. And the vicious crop at the right margin serves as a brake to the outgoing directional lines.

Shattering the composition taboos in this manner is not recommended unless you are very sure of what you are about.

Edgar Degas

Here is another Degas tour de force of things not to do in a composition. Again there is a terrible tangent—the top-hatted character's umbrella is right in the little girl's head. The figure at the extreme left is cropped almost, but not quite, to the point of losing identity. Also, there is a big open path through the center of the picture. And if that is not enough, everyone is looking in different directions. Still it works, and it even sets up a kind of rhythm that seems indicative of the locale. Here is how it goes.

Starting with the man with the jaunty cigar, the eye is led down to his umbrella and to the little girl. We follow her gaze to the left to the other child, to the dog, and to the marginal man, who, along with the background horse, buildings, wall, etc., carry us back to the man with the top hat and cigar. No matter how we may try to do otherwise, our line of vision keeps going around the big circle, leaving a blank Place de la Concorde in the center.

Claude Monet

Claude Monet

Some critics claim Monet lacked the capacity for self-criticism. This conclusion seems questionable, although it is apparent he was often less concerned with composition than with his main interest, color. Certainly a number of the noted Impressionist's paintings are dull designs, and without the force of color they are monotonous. Monet's series of poplar paintings make the point that one aspect of picture making, no matter how important that function may be, can seldom overcome other deficiencies.

In fairness, it should be noted that most of the artist's compositions are not only delights to the eye in color, but also well organized and controlled as to design and mood.

Meindert Hobbema

National Gallery, London

The nature of poplars and the way they are evenly planted along roads in many parts of Europe give rise to a disproportionate number of stilted, unexciting pictures. The noted Dutch artist seemed to have almost as much trouble with poplars as subjects for compositions as did Monet some two hundred years later.

Ben Stahl

New Britain Museum of American Art

Said the artist about his illustration: "It is a terrible picture. Look at the way the man's hand grows out of his shoulder; his foot pokes out of the rim of the barrel; and there is a path right through the center of the composition. This is one of those jobs you do in a hurry, and when you see it later you wish you could take it back so you could destroy it."

This example is included here to make an obvious, but often ignored point: every artist, even the best, signs off on works that seem at the moment satisfactory, yet in retrospect are known to be inadequate. Would we all had the gift of second sight with the time to do something about it.

Floris Verster

Stedelijk Museum, Amsterdam

Not everything of the same size and shape set in a row need be dull. With but slight variations in placement, size, and emphasis Verster shows that a few jugs can be made into an interesting if less than an exciting composition.

139

Balance and unity

Within the universe defined by the perimeter of the picture frame, every viewer seeks to find a sense of balance and unity. When painting a picture, be it soft-focus impression, hard-edged abstraction, realistic illustration, or primitive in approach, the artist must take into consideration the audience's intuitive feeling for perceptual equilibrium. Prominent in the critical language of experts are words such as *spotty, scattered, uncoordinated,* and *confused.* Most relate to balance. Lacking a projection of equipoise, a picture is unlikely to achieve its ultimate goal—harmony and aesthetic unity.

Formal symmetry is seldom a requirement for compositions, although at times such a structure may serve a concept well. Even the most asymmetrical designs usually require balance to avoid the critic's favorite epithets. The only time a picture should appear visually out of balance is when such a condition serves the emotional purpose of the composition. We will address this consideration later.

Imaginary *scales* and *seesaws* are among art teachers' standard devices to demonstrate pictorial balance. In many cases, primarily where the design is based on severe symmetry, such as the Raphael and Cézanne paintings shown on pages 142 and 143, the scale analogy can be readily understood. The comparison is less apparent when dealing with informal balance, or modified symmetry. As much as feasible on the following pages the *classic scale* and the *steelyard* are used to illustrate pictorial balance. However, it is well to keep in mind that compositional equilibrium can depend on representations of depth in space as well as two-dimensional assessment. In addition, we are always dealing with our individual *perception* of weight, a condition somewhat short of precise measurement.

Every element within a picture has the capability of attracting the observer's attention. Experience shows the following general placement factors have a bearing on the degree of attraction each element offers. This in turn becomes a part of the balance quotient.

- An element placed near the picture border tends to have greater importance than the same element placed near the center of the picture space.
- An isolated element has more weight and emphasis than the same element more closely related to others.
- Tangents and lines of opposition generate strong attraction.
- Gradation tends to carry more weight than flat treatment.

Classic scales *(formal balance)—weights measured on arms of equal length from the fulcrum at the center.*

Steelyard *(informal balance)—two arms and weights of unequal measure. The longer arm carries the movable smaller weight as a counterpoise.*

140

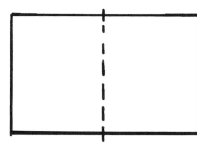 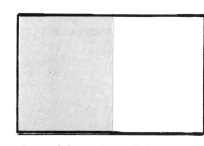 

Intuitively we search for visual balance by dividing the picture space into equal sections. For many pictures the vertical division acts as a fulcrum of a scale.

Areas of close value and of similar size tend to balance each other when on opposite sides of the center axis.

Areas of strong value contrast of similar size on opposing sides of the center axis will usually balance each other.

Dark values are likely to have more attraction and overpower lighter values, even when light area is larger.

Gradations of values have more attraction than flat areas, and therefore they visually carry more weight.

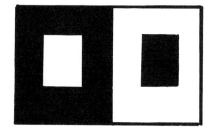 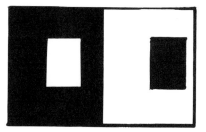

These areas are in balance, but the white square on the black ground creates the illusion of depth—we tend to look through the white window into space. With the black square on the white ground our attention seems to stay on the surface. These properties can be useful in establishing balance.

The dark square shifted close to the picture border generates more attraction and supplies more visual weight to that side. Elements close to the center axis are outweighed by those nearer the margin.

 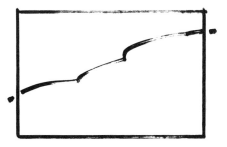

The horizontal axis is the more important division in many landscapes and seascapes.

Some pictures create their own natural axis and visually replace the center axis as the fulcrum.

This is a fine example of pictorial symmetry—the equal balance of picture elements on either side of the center axis. The feeling of serenity and stability are enhanced by the pyramidal structure of the composition.

Raphael

- Strong value and color contrasts have greater attraction than closely related colors and values.
- A foreground element requires less feeling of weight than a similar element in the distance.
- Several elements may be used in combination to visually balance others.
- Balance may be achieved through the use of *values, lines, shape, texture,* and *color.*

Both the vertical and horizontal center lines of the actual picture area are significant in our search for equilibrium. Most of us have a tendency to look at things dead center, and we begin our formulation of visual balance by using an imaginary center line as the pivot. Again, this condition is more clearly evident when dealing with compositions based on symmetry, where the vertical center line is the fulcrum. The horizontal center line is frequently a dominant consideration in landscapes. In any case, it is advisable to observe the obvious, and visually weigh compositional units according to center lines, even when you are building an asymmetrical design.

In some pictures the arrangement of the forms may create a *natural axis* which takes on a life of its own. This type of axis may consist of definite pictorial elements, such as the

Paul Cézanne *Card Players*

Louvre, Paris

This composition by the noted Post-Impressionist is also symmetrical. Although balanced on each side of the vertical axis, the elements are not quite evenly spaced, thus the painting appears a little less formal and rigid than the Madonna on the opposite page. Here again, the picture structure is based on a pyramid.

The artist produced several similar paintings on this theme. Dr. Albert Barnes, a noted critic and collector during the first half of this century, claimed one of Cézanne's Card Players *to be the finest painting ever created.*

crest of a hill against the sky, or it can be an imaginary demarcation that visually serves as a pivotal line. A division of this sort is likely to express the natural environmental balance of the picture elements rather than the actual dimensions of the picture area.

As you examine the illustrations that follow with captions explaining visual balance, remember design equilibrium depends on more than just size and positioning of forms and mass on either side of a fulcrum. Value distributions and color can play major, often interlocking roles. In the long run, of all the components affecting the seesaw of compositional balance, *value*—its placement, size, and density—is usually the most telling factor. Slight adjustments in light or dark areas will usually supply the fine tuning needed to strike the desired critical equilibrium.

In the final analysis, the artist's job in creating a picture is not unlike that of an umpire in a ball game. Most decisions do not come directly out of the rule book, but are based on individual judgment. Visual perception of balance, imbalance, harmony, and disunity always ends up a personal judgment call. And the only way you can call it is the way you see it.

Vincent van Gogh

The simple, classically balanced composition can be found in many types of art. In The Bridge, 1888, *above, the great Post-Impressionist has clearly weighted the scales equally on either side of the vertical centerline. In a similar manner a popular illustrator utilized the same type of modified symmetry to establish visual equilibrium in his pen and ink drawing, below.*

Fred Ludekens

144

John Constable

In this plein air painting, called Study of Tree Trunks, *the noted English landscape artist brought about the feeling of balance based on the visual principle of the steelyard scale. The dark foreground mass that dominates the left side of the composition is effectively offset by the small, but well-placed figure in contrasting value on the right.*

Oskar Kokoschka

 *These two oil paintings by artists with divergent approaches achieve visual balance in a similar manner. As suggested by the diagram of the steelyard scale, in both cases the heavier mass on the right is stabilized by the lighter values and larger areas on the left. Also, the expansive foreground sections are checked by the textural activities in the skies.*

Paul Landry

The lineup of boats and figures in Holiday on the Hudson *creates a strong horizontal path across the center of the composition, keeping the upper and lower portions in balance because of the similarity in size, shape, and color.*

George Luks

A seventeenth century Master and a fine contemporary illustrator employed the same balance principle in solving these compositions. Large foreground elements are held in check by carefully placed opposing areas. (In both cases it will help to imagine the scale in perspective.) In the Fuchs illustration the cropping of the horse's head and the crowding at the upper left serve as a strong attraction and generate the feeling of action. The large, simply stated foreground is countered by the busy sky and the riders at the right. The Ter Borch painting is the reverse of this, with a detailed foreground and subdued background.

Gerard Ter Borch

Bernard Fuchs

This powerfully painted figure is held in balance by the exaggerated treatment of the arms and hands opposed to the dominant, contrasting values in the head and background. Again, it will help to visualize the steelyard scale as if viewed in perspective.

Ben Stahl

An imaginary vertical centerline effectively divides this painting in classic balance. The dominant girl in white at the left is countered by the two smaller dark figures; and the busy clutter of the bottles, glasses, etc., on the table at the right is offset by the distant figures at the left.

Ben Stahl

Milton Avery

Wassily Kandinsky

No matter what the artist's approach, the sense of visual equilibrium is a dominant design factor. Both painters whose work is shown here were obviously not concerned with realistic representation, yet even in the totally abstract Kandinsky picture called St. George No. 3, visual balance is apparent. A case could be made that the more nonrepresentational the treatment, the greater the need for visual stability. Realism and subject matter at times may be used to slur over some design imperatives. Abstraction allows no such crutch.

Stable, secure

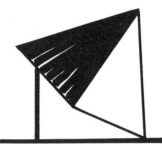

Stable but insecure

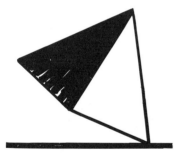

Dangerous

That unbalanced look

Most compositions, even those describing violent action and emotion, are based on visual equilibrium. Also, many and varied pictures are built on a definite structure such as a circle, square, or triangle. The Raphael and Cézanne paintings on pages 142 and 143, as well as Picasso's *Guernica,* shown on page 197, are all based on the solid, stable structure of the pyramid. There are times, however, when such a secure foundation, positively balanced, may impede the desired effect.

Using diagrams similar to those at the left, Harold Von Schmidt used to make this point about stability. We know, he would say, a pyramid resting squarely on its base is the most secure structure man can construct. However, if you tip that pyramid up, as we may do in a picture, so it rests on one point, and prop it in place, we sense it may not fall, but we'd think twice before we would walk under it. If you take away the support, we know that thing is going to fall, and anybody would be a damn fool to go near it. Something violent is sure to happen.

As creatures of our environment we are all conditioned to situations of possible peril. Although civilization has dulled instincts that once were essential in protecting our kind, we are nonetheless keenly alert to certain danger signals. When we see something is out of balance we know there is the possibility it may fall. Falling means trouble, with things out of control. This implies confusion and often unmanageable speed. Both conditions spell *action* and *danger.* And these conditions may be exactly what an artist wishes to convey in a picture. When a visual concept calls for excitement, speed, or instability, an unbalanced composition may be the best answer.

Peter Helck and Bernie Fuchs used this principle effectively in their illustrations for quite different reasons. In the picture of the speeding train, the crowding of all the weight and emphasis at the right margin generates a feeling of speed and excitement. In the Fuchs picture, the child cowering in the corner, holding his mother's knee, suggests timidity and shyness. Here the danger is psychological and emotional, rather than physical. In both instances a visually unbalanced look supports the picture concept.

Peter Helck

Bernard Fuchs

Pierre Bonnard

Some pictures, no matter how you try to reconcile their components, never seem satisfactory in the balance department. This little modified L-shaped painting, called The Review, *is one of them. I have studied it in color, which is delightful, and in black and white—turned it upside down and sideways. No matter how I look at it, my internal scale always registers a decided list to port. Only the abnormally large initials in the lower right corner keep the picture from tilting in its frame. P.B. must have felt the same way, for it was not his custom to identify his paintings with such a strident signature.*

Value—the lightness or darkness of things

Nothing has such an effect on the merits of a rendering as the treatment of values. The intellectual concept of light and dark, gradations of white to black on the familiar gray number scale, and the cardinal characteristics of value in color are simple enough to understand. But *how* value is controlled in a composition makes the difference between the great and the ordinary in a picture.

In realistic painting, probably the most difficult aspect of value and color to comprehend is our extreme limitation in relating what we can see to what is possible to achieve with any type of pigment. If the colors and values we discern in nature were equated as ten on a scale of one to ten, that which we could reasonably match with paint would register around the low side of four. If you doubt the validity of this assumption, try a simple experiment. Hold at arm's length against the daytime sky a piece of the whitest paper you can find. Even on a dull, overcast day you will be amazed at how gray your white paper is compared to the brilliance of the sky.

The same kind of relationship exists with all values and colors we use, no matter how extensive our palette. Von Schmidt once identified forty-three different shades of green he saw while taking a short stroll near his Connecticut studio. No doubt Von's educated eye and skilled hand could approximate in paint many of the gradations, but he could suggest only a few in any given picture.

The point is, there is no way—or need—to match what we see. That is not what art is all about. The best we can ever hope for is to establish a relationship that suggests an illusion of something seen or imagined. Pictures are not reality. Some artists labor long and hard at *deceiving the eye* to make us think we are seeing the real thing and not a rendering. Often we can admire the technical skill and craftsmanship involved in such exercises, but in truth the result of even the most clever interpretations will never "fool a dog."*

It is the function of values to control the individual parts so the picture can meld into the kind of unity Reynolds refers to in the quotation above. How do you go about this, and what are the specific considerations necessary to control values? Basically there are three factors involved:

1 The local color of an object—the red of a red painted barn, the green of a tree's leaves, etc.

*This refers to an old artists' story, the origin of which probably goes back to the Romans. One version goes like this: Two gallery visitors are admiring a meticulously detailed *trompe-l'oeil* painting of a tree in a park. (Some raconteurs specify the subject as a fire hydrant.) Said one, "What a remarkable work! No matter where you view it—up close or across the room—it looks exactly like the real thing." "Yes," replied the other, "but it won't fool a dog."

Everything has a value, and that value is visually relative to the environment in which it is seen. As demonstrated here, the gray rectangles are the same size, shape and value, but they appear different because of their background.

2 The light and shadow that fall on an object—the sunny side of a tree or rock have different values than the shadow sides.

3 The atmosphere—values and colors appear less contrasting and intense in the distance than they do nearby; this is called *aerial perspective.*

Light and dark are relative qualities. There are no absolutes involved, even if your concern is merely to duplicate as closely as possible the values and colors you see. Isolating your "slice of nature" within the confines of the picture space requires many adjustments to satisfy the eye and project the illusion of the scene. Space, scale, and our vast spectrum of vision allow an acceptance and harmony to exist in a natural setting that is not possible to achieve in a reduced facsimile.

An old art class axiom states: In painting, *light is produced by sacrifice.* Many such all-inclusive phrases are open to challenge, if not ridicule, but this one is not to be faulted. The only way a portion of our gray white paper (gray, when compared to the sky) can suggest brilliance is by placing it in opposition to strong, contrasting darks. Observation proves a small, light area looks brighter when surrounded by a large mass of dark than a large area of white does when it is opposed to a small area of dark. With the gradation of either the light or dark there is a reduction in brilliancy. These simple facts, used in conjunction with a disciplined hand and an intuitive eye comprise the strongest part of the artist's arsenal when battling to control values. No other engagement in the process of painting is so vital to the final effectiveness of the picture.

One of the battles the beginner must learn to wage is to draw what he sees, and not what he thinks he sees. There is often quite a difference. We know a telephone pole, for example, is about the same color and value from top to bottom. Yet, often that is not what we actually observe. As this somewhat exaggerated sketch suggests, when we see the pole isolated against a darker background it may appear much lighter than the portion exhibited against a light sky. It requires courage to make a visual statement that intellectually we know to be wrong.

Albin Henning

This same size charcoal sketch conveys a great deal with little more than three values. Notice how much mood and feeling are suggested with a minimum of details and definition.

monumental, regal

calm, peaceful

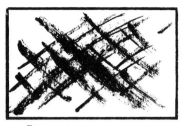

conflict, action

sadness, despair

explosive, excited

gloom, mystery

Creating mood

Just as every picture of every quality and classification is, by its nature, organized into some kind of a design, so too every picture strives to generate a mood. Anyone who seriously studies paintings will soon be aware that values in a composition play a powerful part in evoking emotion. The *light* and *dark* of things is the basis of what we see. As inhabitors of earth depending on the sun for life, we are all acutely attuned to the ebb and flow of day and night—light and dark—and every nuance of grayed color in between peals an emotional response as predictable as the clock striking the hour. Values of themselves, however, do not always control the mood of a picture. They must work hand in hand with other elements to assure a desired result.

Almost as potent as the force of values in a composition are the abstract shapes and line directions such as those diagrammed in the margins. In many cultures such symbols have a meaningful effect. They should not, however, be thought of as universal. Symbols, like road signs, must be learned. Some non-Western societies may interpret these seemingly palpable representations quite obliquely. For example, many Orientals do not associate black with gloom or despair; instead they consider white as the color of mourning. In ancient Rome blue was a token of death. Time, fashion, and intellectual symbols change. But you can be assured if you use the totemism shown here, Western viewers, at least, will grant them positive acceptance.

Two other considerations that affect a picture's mood are subject matter and color. Subject is of importance only if you are dealing with some kind of realism. In any case, it is less influential than values, abstract shapes, or symbols. As to color, the artist's treatment and the viewer's reaction are so personal in this area that general procedures are just about impossible to categorize. The most consequential color factor affecting the mood of a painting is its key, which, of course, largely depends on the values used.

156

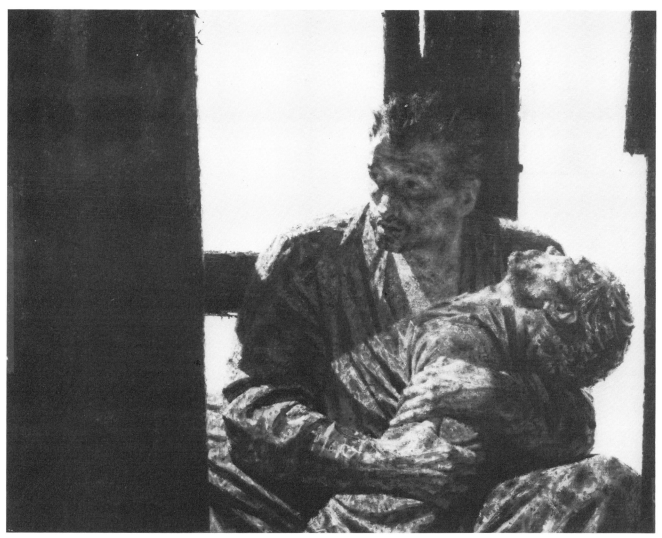

Joseph Hirsch

This fine painting, called Deposition, *embodies compelling value patterns and contrasts with a forceful abstract design. All elements work together to portray a poignant sense of pathos and dignity. Hirsch's original concept was to represent a battle-weary soldier comforting his wounded buddy. Later he decided to de-emphasize the military aspect and strive for a more universal condition. The dominant vertical thrust of the design, combined with the forceful value pattern, establish the desired mood of nobility rather than one of sadness or defeat.*

Ben Stahl

Ben Stahl

Few painters work with the emotional exuberance of the indefatigable Mr. Stahl. His instinct for the sweeping, telling line in combination with undulating values, gives his work a compelling power. Seldom will he depart from the simple, straightforward visual statement. In these examples, notice the strong use of the symbols discussed in the text. In the landscape above the tranquil horizontal emphasis is dominant. In the figure at the right, the upward thrust of nobility and spirituality cannot be challenged. And all of this is embellished with beautifully sensitive color.

Ben Stahl

John Hancock Mutual Life Insurance Company

This is a near-classic example of combining dramatic value contrasts with strong, opposing diagonals to create the feeling of conflict, and excitement.

Where does all this lead? Simply, the artist who wishes to establish a specific visual emotion must orchestrate the right type and mixture of values, abstract shapes, symbols, subject matter, and color within the composition. If you are able to combine these into appropriate balance you can be reasonably sure of creating your desired picture mood.

Unfortunately, the painter's lot is seldom simple. The linkage of all the telling ingredients in a picture's makeup is rarely obvious. Not often will you find concepts and compositions that dovetail with the isolated iconology diagrammed here. Many themes are varied and complex, and their compositional solution demands subtle, if not far-reaching adjustments to convey the desired feeling. A rolling landscape, for instance, ideally would be identified with the tranquil symbol of dominant horizontal lines; yet an ominous, agitated sky or up-thrusting trees might offer the kind of interest you want. Immediately you are faced with a conflict of opposites. Don't despair. Such counterpoint can be stimulating, and if deftly handled the dichotomy can be of interest and excitement. The skillful etching by Anders Zorn shown on page 160 is a case in

Anders Zorn

Exceptions to the usual approach can be made to work, and work effectively, as demonstrated here. The dark shapes and the dominant dark value pattern in this etching suggest intimacy and warmth, rather than gloom and doom.

point. The massive dark shapes and strong shadow pattern, although dominant, do not project a mood of gloom or mystery. Rather, the feeling is one of warmth and intimacy, brought about mainly by the subject matter and the well-planned light areas.

You must be cautious when dealing with symbols and values that are inappropriate to each other or run counter to the thrust of your concept. Randomly pursuing such a course is on the order of shooting at a target while blindfolded. You might hit something, but it probably won't be what you had in mind. Painting in a realistic or naturalistic manner requires uniting the correct symbols, subject, color, and intrinsic values, if you hope to score an emotional bull's eye.

Keying and limiting values

After studying the works of Titian, Tintoretto, Veronese, Rembrandt and Rubens, the British painter, Joshua Reynolds, two hundred years ago observed the following regarding the Masters' application of values:

"A general practice appeared to be to allow not above a quarter of the picture for light, including in this portion both the principal and secondary lights; another quarter to be as dark as possible and the remaining half kept in mezzo-tint or half shadow. . . . Rubens appears to have admitted rather more light than a quarter and Rembrandt much less, scarce an eighth; by this conduct Rembrandt's light is extremely brilliant, but it costs too much; the rest of the picture is sacrificed to this one object."

It is difficult to disagree with Sir Joshua's conclusion. Many Masters works conform to such a formula, with the result that a steady diet of their paintings—excepting Rembrandt's—tend to be monotonous viewing in the area of lighting and color. Some contemporary paintings may have similar value proportions, but it is doubtful many were conceived on such a regimented basis. Whatever else may be said about twentieth century painting, it is seldom dull or predictable. The turmoil that has embroiled the art world in the last one hundred years has succeeded in sweeping away most of the old standards of light and color.

Today almost anything goes. Nonetheless, there are a few watchwords to heed. These have to do with keeping your picture in *key*. In painting, as in great music, harmony and aesthetic fulfillment are likely to be achieved only when the performance is in the right key. Some of the musical notes in pictures are the values and colors you use. They will carry out their task most effectively if they are held within a controlled range.

Why should this be? Available to us is a spread of values from black to white, and any art store can supply us with a near rainbow of tubed colors. Why not use them any way we want?

If you are working in an abstract, nonobjective manner, or possibly depicting a scene influenced by a manmade environment with, say, psychedelic lighting, you can be as arbitrary as you wish to achieve your results. But, if you wish to imply some kind of realism in your work, then restraint will be necessary. Here's why.

The sun and its reflected light from the moon are the world's cardinal sources of illumination. Therefore everything we see in nature is always bathed in a consistent light. Whatever hue, value or chroma we see will appear in harmony with everything else. It will be in *key*. That key will vary according to the quality of light; but be it in the full glare of the sun, in fog, haze, drizzle, or in the glow of a waning moon, the scene will never look inconsistent. Even with most manmade electrical illumination designed to serve as a substitute for daylight, a similar harmony usually prevails. To deny this fact in a picture is to move towards the visually unreal and unbelievable.

In general, most artists tend to contain their pictures in one of four major value keys—high, middle, low, and full range. As each identification suggests, the majority of the values used in the picture are limited to that portion of the value scale. The high-key painting mainly contains values from the light side of the scale; the low-key picture is based largely on the dark end, etc. Keep in mind that a picture need not be to-

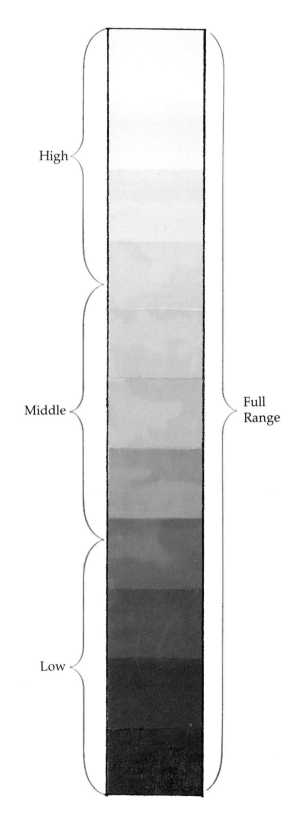

High

Middle

Low

Full Range

A

B

C

D

tally limited to the values in the prescribed range. At times a few accents reaching up or down in the value scale may be necessary. Such lack of purity is permissible so long as the overall harmony remains intact.

The full range picture, though it may sound the simplest, is likely to cause trouble because the middle values become difficult to control. Pictures, as has been noted several times, are not reality. And we are limited in our means to duplicate what we see. We must project an illusion. To do so requires controlling the relationships of all elements. Even if we can keep our full range picture in a harmony throughout, some part of the illusion is likely to suffer because our palette and range of values cannot match what is seen in nature.

Largely for these reasons many artists find it advantageous to limit themselves to three or four values even when working on a painting covering a full range. Using just three or four values forces simplification—everything must be reduced to a light, dark or middle value. It is amazing how much power and directness you can achieve when painting in this manner. Although this type of thinking is helpful in all mediums, watercolorists in particular benefit from it. As Claude Croney says, "It's a lot easier to make what's light, light and what's dark, dark—and not to worry about subtle nuances. Aiming at a few big targets, you're more likely to hit them."

When painting it is also wise to keep in mind and identify your lightest lights and your darkest darks. Both areas should be controlled and limited. Harvey Dunn, by way of Howard Pyle, had some excellent advice on this score. "Always keep a shot in your locker," he said. By this he meant to save your extreme lights and darks for the few spots where they would do the most good. In this way, for instance, the final highlight in an eye can become the powerful visual force you want it to be. Combining such value control with similar judicial handling of color can make your painting sparkle.

Rhythm and movement

Our instinct for rhythm, be it the audio-inspired, toe-tapping variety, or the visual repetition in design, is said to be a direct response to the pulse of life, our heartbeat. Whatever the cause, its persuasiveness is ever present. As in music—or the melody of words, poetry—visual rhythms can run the range from quiet and smooth to violent, vibrant, and staccato. In every case, the type used must be appropriate to the desired effect.

Visual rhythms are created by repeating identifiable picture elements, usually shapes, lines, values, and colors. Dull, regular repetition is seldom effective. To sustain interest pictures must have variety. A rhythmical flow of similar units offering some variation adds spice to a design. Such a flow is also a major means of producing a feeling of visual movement.

John Singer Sargent

Isabella Stewart Gardner Museum, Boston

The best way to tune in on the effect of rhythm in pictures is to study examples of its use. The diagrams and examples at the left suggest a variety of visual rhythms. At the top in A, the simple repetition of lines and dots, as often seen in fabric and wallpaper, clearly projects a definite cadence with predictable, usually monotonous movement. The illustrations below show how this same principle can be used in a variety of picture approaches.

Figure B is a detail of a fifteenth century woodcut by an unknown artist. Notice the use of the rhythmic lines in the drapery of the dress that creates a feeling of movement and tension. This is echoed by the frieze-type design in the background. In C, the twentieth century illustrator, Fred Ludekens, utilizes the repetitious cone shapes of pines along with the bleached limbs of a fallen tree to serve a similar purpose in this detail of one of his pen and ink drawings. The watercolor cloud effect in D incorporates the same kind of thinking in a less precise manner.

The illusion of movement in a picture can be created in a number of ways. Closely related to rhythm is what is referred to as *tension*. As used by artists, the word goes a bit beyond its dictionary definition, "the act of stretching or straining." Generally it is taken to mean the condition in a composition that sets up an attraction or repulsion of elements. This can be accomplished through the placement and thrust of lines, values, shapes, color, and even textures. Tension in this regard is

Here is a beautifully rendered painting expressing a strong sense of rhythm and tension. The vertical angle and thrust of the dancer relative to the horizontal grouping of figures in the background, as well as her relationship to the picture's right margin, create tension and movement. Notice the staccato positioning of the musicians seated along the wall. Their even placement, nicely interrupted by one empty chair serving like a musical rest, supplies rhythm that echoes the cadence of the dance. The guitars hanging on the wall repeat the rhythm. Such a painting you can hear as well as see.

163

Frank Webb

In this fine watercolor called The Depot, Duluth, *a feeling of movement and rhythm is generated by the repetition of the angular light shapes deftly scattered throughout the composition. There is no strong center of interest; rather an overall feeling of excitement and upward thrust is established.*

an important factor in movement. Basically it is the viewer's sense of a relationship existing in the positions of two or more obvious compositional elements. The picture's borders often play a part in creating tension, as do forms whose positions generate near-parallel thrust, or areas of tangency or near tangency. As with rhythms and other facets of design, the best way to understand visual tension is through example. In illustrations that follow, the use of tension will be pointed out where it is apparent.

The center of interest

People who spend more time talking about pictures than they do creating them advance a number of theories about the way the viewer is visually lured into the intricate web of a composition. These are spelled out in terms such as *points of entry, secondary entry, eye paths, foils, traps,* and other buzzwords. These ideas may be valid, but their most practical use is in making impressive conversation at gallery gatherings. For the working artist such verbalizing is of debatable value.

The fine points of how each of us "*gets into*" a picture are as suspect as a sighting of the Loch Ness monster. When viewing a painting, any painting, do our eyes begin at the bottom border and look upward? Do we start at the upper left and run down and across as if we were reading a book? Or, does our

Albin Henning

gaze zero in on the picture's geometric center? Who knows? And what difference does it make?

Each composition is a universe in itself, and it must manifest sufficient appeal through its shapes, values, colors, patterns, textures, technical facility, or subject matter to persuade the viewer to stop and appraise the work with more than a passing glance. Just how and where we start our study of a composition is of no consequence. Once started, however, we can hope the artist has so organized the design that our eyes will find movement, excitement, and an arresting area of interest.

Discounting the haphazard procedures of action painters, dribblers, and others of the Abstract Expressionist movement, it is fair to speculate the majority of pictures are conceived with a definite center of interest in mind. Certainly, compositions that aim to communicate forcefully are likely to be formulated on that basis. This is not to suggest that every picture need have an avowed, or even a discernible focal point. There are numerous examples of paintings by prestigious artists where a clear-cut center of interest is as difficult to find as a parking place on Main Street. In such pictures, the artist's apparent intentions were to avoid dramatic impact in favor of a visual totality. This approach works satisfactorily most often in landscapes, particularly those suggesting a panoramic view.

On the other hand, compositions designed to emphasize a particular area should use every means to make that point a

Composition for my father was an intuitive thing. "I put things," he said, "where they look right." Upon analysis, his compositional instinct rated high scores. This illustration is a case in point.

Here the center of interest is the bandaged head of the soldier on the stretcher. No matter where you start to look into the picture your eye is attracted to that area. In the foreground the trench ladder, the diagonally placed board, and the rifles take you to the lead stretcher bearer and back along the stretcher to the white bandages. If your gaze tries to go back across the helmets to the figures following at the left, it is stopped like a period at the end of a sentence by the vertical spike of the bayonet fixed to the slung rifle. Inexorably your eye path is forced downward to pick up again the foreground directional lines that take you back on a circular course to the center of interest. Notice how a sense of movement is established by the rhythmic positioning of the soldiers' legs.

165

El Greco, *View of Toledo*

The Metropolitan Museum of Art, New York

The center of interest in this painting is neither overpowering nor compelling. The moody sky, complemented by the mystery of the foreground, claims almost as much viewer attention as the important structures in the distance. Everything is harmoniously in place. It is the overall effect within a beautifully flowing design that marks this work as a masterpiece.

telling and significant part of the picture. This is the stage position for the star, the plot, and essence of the picture. But don't overdo it. No matter what your approach—be it realistic, impressionistic, abstract, or whatever, there should be no more than *one major* center of interest.

The astute observer can correctly claim certain pictures, usually murals and other outsized paintings, often enjoy success without the burden of such restrictions. (A case in point is the Rockwell mural shown on page 35.) With study you can discover many compositions like this that appear guilty of such design malfeasance are innocent if the work is viewed in definable segments. Under most circumstances, however, pictures containing more than a single significant focal center are flawed.

Why?

The best answer is that no one can demonstrate otherwise. As with language, the simple, direct statement is clearer, and carries greater meaning than one that tries to say several

Pieter Bruegel, *The Wedding Banquet*

things at once. Pictures that try to scatter their emphasis and say, in equally demanding tones, more than one thing at a time, invariably succeed in saying little. As watercolorist Frank Webb succinctly states, "There is no place in painting for optical democracy."*

Many pictures have important secondary areas of interest; some have several. Such dilution inevitably reduces impact. The problem is not a matter of limiting the composition to single-element status. Pictures with multiple subjects can be effectively controlled so that a single focal center is overwhelmingly dominant.

In much of the preceding text we have alluded to methods by which the observer's attention can be directed to the composition's center of interest. Value contrasts, directional lines, placement, and color are some of the means the artist can use to emphasize the importance of a given area. The determination of *what* that area will be should have its genesis at the concept stage. At the beginning of your picture planning you should determine *what* you want to stress and *what* you want to say.

In several illustrations that follow, the centers of interest and the manner in which they function within the compositions are discussed. Studying these examples will help you understand this critical part of picture making.

*From Watercolor Energies, *by Frank Webb, published by North Light © 1983*

Many of the Flemish Master's paintings are based on a scattered panoramic effect, with no obvious single center of interest. This picture is one of several exceptions. Here the foreground men serving the soup clearly star in the scene because of their positioning, size, and color. In addition, the directional lines of the tables, the grouping of the seated people, and the activity on the left side of the composition all lead the viewer's attention to them. The repetitious shapes sustain the feeling of life and movement.

167

Paul Cézanne

This painting is typical of many Cézanne's landscapes that do not have a prominent center of interest. It must be viewed as a totality in which all areas claim nearly equal emphasis. There is a remarkable relationship of colors that suggests reality and the essence of the place far better than photographic realism.

Point of view

Merging like speeding cars traveling in the same direction, parallel to each other on a narrowing highway are the twin compositional considerations, *center of interest* and *point of view*. At an early stage in the planning process these two forces must synchronize, and jointly propel the picture into a specific statement. As you conceptualize your composition the first decisions usually contend with *what* you wish to emphasize. Next in order is the *how* of viewing it. Will it be most effective to look down on the scene? Or look up at it? Should you attack straight on from the front? Or, would an oblique approach have greater appeal?

The outstanding illustrator and sometimes teacher, Robert Fawcett, was fascinated with drawing and the early phase of picture making. He once concocted an exercise for his students that dealt forthrightly with the problem of picture point of view. The approach also considered a number of other pertinent aspects of compositional planning. Although Fawcett's approach is that of an illustrator, the thinking involved is relevant for all types of representational pictures. What follows is a portion of that exercise, including sketches and the written explanation by the artist describing his procedure.

Camille Pissarro

Assignment:

Translate this story situation into a picture in any medium you wish. Allow a minimum of technique to intrude between you and the concept as you see it.

The scene is a country newspaper office and the editor, a genial old character of about sixty-five, is leaning back in a swivel chair to impart words of wisdom to a young reporter who stands beside him. No change in the interior of the office has taken place for at least forty years and the whole mood is warm and nostalgic. The time is a late August afternoon and the picture interest is conveyed by the contrast of the two characters. Allow your observation or imagination to supply whatever details you think will make the scene more real, even though the manuscript does not describe it in detail.*

The first decision is how you will view the scene—this decision must be made simply, directly, decisively.

The three main choices are:

1 To stand where you can see [the figures] equally. This will result in a flat composition.
2 Stand behind the reporter, looking directly at the old editor.
3 Stand behind the editor and his desk looking towards the reporter.

*This portion of the assignment reprinted with permission of R.D. Cortina Company, Inc.

Many landscapes, even plein air panoramic approaches such as this, contain a definite focal area. The center of interest need not be overpowering. Here Pissarro gently nudges the viewer's attention to the key area. Notice how the curve of the roadway, the strong dark edge of the foreground bushes, as well as the background buildings and trees direct our gaze to the two women walking toward us. Our glance may first be attracted to the sky and the crest of the distant hill, but leisurely we are drawn down into and around the entire composition.

Equal emphasis on figures.

The decision should be made by consulting the manuscript. (a) Who is the most important character in the story? (b) Look at him and allow the other character to act as a foil. (c) If equally important, then #1 (above) is indicated, which divides the attention equally.

The second decision is how much of the entire picture space the figures will occupy.

1 They should occupy around two-thirds [of the space] since this is a figure situation and the human element is paramount.

2 Outline the figures' positions and shade to be sure they do not float loosely within the picture space. The total figure area should fit pleasantly, easily into the outside rectangle, without crowding and without becoming lost. If one figure goes over the outside edge, the other should remain within the enclosure.

3 The space left should be able to accommodate all the atmosphere.

Look past the reporter at the editor.

Note—*Equidistant view* suggests flat decorative composition, with little depth.

—*Reporter, back view* suggests [to me] window behind the editor, maybe trees outside and small town. Window blind partly pulled down, etc. (Watch light source in this one.)

—*Editor, back view* suggests entry door behind reporter, but light source from out of picture [at] right.

The second stage places the scenes. This is best done by visiting a newspaper office of the type [if possible] and carefully observing all the small things in the editor's office which you expected, and also the details and equipment which you never thought of. Take a camera along as an aid to your memory, but make no attempt to alter your composition unless [you find] yours was radically wrong.

Look past the editor at the reporter.

All the details should be taken out and fitted into your picture idea where they operate best compositionally. Concentrate, while in the office, on making an *inventory,* by quick sketches or photos.

Back in the studio boil down all you have seen or photographed into a simple pattern to fit the space around the figures, but in a way that does not interfere with them—merely supports and supplements them. Rearrange everything to this end, and limit yourself to the minimum amount. Don't crowd the composition with too much stuff. Suggest by a part rather than draw the whole. Some can *cut into* the figure space if necessary.

Some of the things that might be present: Rolltop desk, clock on the wall, calendar, pastepot, galley proofs, scissors, typewriters, account and record books, a small scale, electric fan, typefaces pinned to wall, stamping machine, bare wood floor, rubber stamps, miscellaneous papers (some on floor), wastebasket (filled to top), ashtrays, tray of paper clips, phone, paper press, etc.

All of these things and more you will see, but *only use what you need* in the composition. Choose objects which by their shape and character quickly say "newspaper office."

All these should be old-fashioned. Sometimes stretch a point to *keep everything in character.*

At the same time consider the characters carefully and take whatever means you need to document them.

Imagine the situation—See the young reporter, hot, with jacket over his arm, attentive but not obsequious. It is a small office, everybody is on friendly terms. His hat on, but pushed back would be typical.

The editor is short and rotund, pleasantly stern, leaning back relaxedly in a swivel chair. His tie is also loose, and he holds in one hand something they are discussing or that he is working on.

Then imagine facial characteristics. He wears glasses, he has a mustache (or not), eyeshade, cigar, pencils in vest pocket. His face is red from the heat, but the effect is good-tempered.

Work all these into one simple composition, altering and changing slightly anything which seems wrong, or which jars the eye.

Third stage—Spotting and creating picture interest.
Final stage is the overall spotting [of darks] to keep the picture alive.

- Use both large and small areas.
- See that they are nicely patterned with each other.
- Use to clarify the composition.
- Use to isolate or draw attention to the points of interest.
- Avoid having them confuse a point of interest (such as a profile)—use to isolate a profile.
- See them first in terms of light and dark—later in terms of color.

Finally, *forget all technique,* and with the foregoing procedure established, dig in to make the picture as real and satisfying, by any means at your disposal, as you can. Nothing that you have put down cannot be changed, and getting over and *completely realizing the idea should take precedence over everything else.**

With permission of The New Britain Museum of American Art which houses these notes and sketches of Robert Fawcett.

Henri de Toulouse-Lautrec *The Ringmaster*

The Art Institute of Chicago, Joseph Winterbotham Collection

There is no question the ringmaster dominates this composition. His compelling dark, silhouetted shape cannot be ignored. At the same time, the position of his arm and the angle of his whip lead us directly to the prancing horse. And the horse and rider meld into the rhythmic arcs of the seats and the edge of the ring. These in turn propel us in a circular course around the picture and back to the focal area. The action of the man, the angle of the horse, and the repetitious curves generate a sense of movement and life. The sparkling circus colors of the original add to the feeling of place.

Color and composition

Color, particularly in its more scientific aspects, can be a long and engrossing study. All artists should learn all they can about it, although some of the complexities of the properties of light seem better left to the physicist. A number of theoretical painting principles have ardent supporters among artists, and their arguments can be persuasive. In the long run, however, theory must slide into the back seat when it comes to the effectiveness of personal interpretation based on intuition. Few expert theorists are noted for the quality of color in their pictures. But many artists with minimal knowledge of the subject are renowned for their color.

When using color to help solve compositional problems, it will surely help if you are conversant with the three fundamental dimensions of color: *hue, value,* and *intensity.* Even more important is to be aware of the effects of one color on another—its warm and cool characteristics, how to lighten and darken, as well as how to mix and gray. Detailed analysis of color is beyond the purpose of this book. Such a study should be addressed as a separate subject. Much detailed information is available. Your local library is a good place to start.

Color, and each individual's reaction to it, is so personal that generalities are meaningless. What color you use, in what quantity, when and where, warm or cool, bright or subdued, is such a matter of taste and spontaneous judgment there is seldom a way to preordain a successful outcome. Trust in your own judgment, tempered by experience and practice, is the only operational rule I can offer. This will not guarantee results, but its unpredictability can be exciting. When successful, the feeling can be mighty rewarding.

In most cases the color you use will neither secure triumph nor inflict defeat on your concept and composition. It can enhance both, or it may detract from both. It can even override both and become a separate visual entity. In such cases you may have an unexpected but satisfying result. Like a happy accident in a watercolor, it is nice when it happens, but you rarely know just how it came about.

On the following pages we will analyze a number of diverse paintings to demonstrate the role color plays in developing a picture's concept and composition. The discussion will not be restricted to color considerations. Rather, it will deal with the total picture, covering as much as possible all the ramifications of composition we have already discussed. As with every painting, success depends on a harmonious unification of all the parts. Color is but one component.

The designated role of the illustrator is to play second fiddle to the author's lead. Illustrations should support and embellish the written word, set the story's mood, evoke interest, and decorate the printed page. Pictures created on such a basis should always be considered in relation to how well they fulfill their assigned task. Let's examine this illustration with such a premise in mind.

In this instance, the artist was sent a manuscript by a discerning art director whose only instructions were to deliver the picture by a certain date. The story, an updated King Lear situation, had to do with an elderly farmer whose children were squabbling among themselves about how to divide the land when their father died. Much of the narrative had to do with the sad and dejected old man as he contemplated the bitter ways of life. His one loyal friend was his dog.

Obviously, the old man is the key picture element and he must be shown in an environment that will identify the locale and project the overall mood. Compositionally, to help achieve the physiological implications, the lone figure was placed in a trapped position at the intersection of two strong opposing design forces—the vertical thrust of the dark tree and the stone wall running horizontally in the background. The figure's drooping pose is echoed by the downward sweep of the overhanging branches.

The middle ground is handled simply with three well-placed scratching chickens to establish the farmyard setting. The crate and pan of water in the foreground set the scene, help establish visual balance, and direct the eye towards the center of interest. The position of the dog and the angle of the arms lead our gaze inexorably to the man's head. If our attention starts to wander to the right along the wall, we are gently nudged back towards the bench by the placement of the white hens.

As the diagram indicates, the painting is an example of the effective use of limited values. The scope is full range. How-

Albin Henning

ever, the picture employs only four values, the lightest of
which is so sparsely used that the burden is really carried by
three tones. The color is also reserved and restricted in keeping with the subdued mood. The basic palette includes: viri-
dian, yellow ochre, touches of cadmium red, ultramarine
blue, black, and white. The medium was oil.

The result is a picture thoughtfully conceived, efficiently
composed, and forthrightly handled. It is a telling illustration
that goes beyond the story it was made to support. It stands
on its own as an effective painting.

Harvey Dunn

Walt Reed Collection, Illustration House, South Norwalk, Connecticut

*This simple composition is deceptively well de-
signed. All of the spatial divisions are varied in
size and shape, while the interest areas are contained within the boat by an intriguing light
and dark pattern. Because of his unobstructed
position our attention is first attracted to the
man seated in the stern, but our eyes do not remain there. Almost immediately our gaze shifts
to the forceful tangent at the right margin.
Then we are pulled upward to the area of the
limp sail and down to the man under the awn-
ing. All the busyness of the painting is concentrated in the boat as it floats in a near stagnant
sea, blending indistinguishably with the sky.
Harvey Dunn's foremost concern was always
with values and color, but almost all of his
paintings were built on a strong design concept.*

Harvey Dunn was a big, rawboned lumberjack of a man. To
those who knew him he was larger than life, a man of legendary stature whose influence as an artist and teacher far tran-
scends his own time. A student of Howard Pyle, Dunn looked
upon art—and illustration in particular—as a noble calling to
be approached by the practitioner with a spiritual fervor. A
rugged individualist, he could be warm and compassionate to
all who tried, but when artistic integrity was in question he
was as uncompromising as the climate of his native Dakota
prairie.

Not one to readily accept a secondary role for the illustrator,
Dunn felt pictures were as important, or more so, than most
writer's words. At times his cavalier attitude towards authors
led to amusing difficulties. An example, told to me with un-
abashed glee by my father, goes this way.

Dunn was assigned a story by a national magazine. The
scene he decided to illustrate had to do with a man driving a
wagon pulled by four horses. The text was specific in stating
the two lead animals were white and the other team was dark
in color. Such details were not the type of thing to cause Mr.
Dunn much concern. In his final painting he apparently felt

Harvey Dunn

Walt Reed Collection, Illustration House, South Norwalk, Connecticut

the composition and pattern worked better by having the dark horses in the foretraces.

In due course the picture was delivered, accepted by the editors, and eventually published. Sometime later an observant reader wrote to the magazine's offices pointing out the discrepancy between the story and the illustration. The editors indignantly forwarded the letter to the artist for an explanation. After reading the message, Dunn scrawled a single sentence across the bottom of the page and mailed it back. He had written: "The author was in error. H.D."

Here the flowing, circular grouping of the figures is nicely contained within a dark, almost black pattern that nearly surrounds them. Notice how the darks are spotted to move our attention rhythmically around the picture. The stripes on the dress of the foreground woman lead us from her head down to her feet. Her dark toed shoes point directly to the middle woman, and we follow her gaze across the clapboards to the third lady at the left. Around and around our eye travels, finding bits of interest in every section of the composition.

Howard Pyle

The burning galleon, with its dominant color and intriguing shape, is the unmistakable center of interest in this powerful painting. The curve of the dark, overlapping sail of the foreground boat directs our attention to the pirates at the left. The subtle moon just above the horizon moves our eye back to the stern of the large vessel. On about the second pass of this designed circular course we spy the boarding party almost hidden between the parallel masts of the two small boats. The matching thrusts of these oblique masts stand in opposition to the galleon, and so generate a feeling of conflict, movement, and tension. The quiet, harmonious color scheme serves to make the mischief at hand more unexpected and treacherous.

Harold Von Schmidt

Composition was one of Von's favorite topics. Almost any picture he viewed sparked comments about eye movement and color. Many of his own compositions were predicated on what he called a "figure 8" pattern, or "the skyrocket effect." The white bull painting (above) is an example of his figure 8 design. This is how it goes: Because of size, placement, color, and value, the forepart of the bull and the rider above him are the compelling center of interest. Led by the thrust and angle of the bull's head our eye travels up the cowboy's green slicker to his upraised arm and the coiled rope. We then jump to the white patch of clouds at the upper left, and down to the raised arm of the rider in the mid-distance. This brings us back to the bull. Next time around our eye may travel up the foreground horse's neck and head, out to the right, and across the dark edge of the lowering cloud. Here our gaze is forced down to the lone, nearly silhouetted rider at the head of the herd. Now we follow the line of cattle back to the center of interest, completing the figure 8.

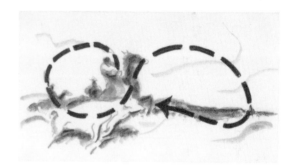

Von, no doubt, knew about the golden mean, but he never talked about it. In this composition it is interesting to note that a crucial area coincides with the perfect ratio we discussed earlier. The coordinates intersect at the near cowboy's raised arm. It is doubtful this placement was mathematically premeditated.

This is one of Von Schmidt's illustrations based on his "skyrocket" concept. The pony's head serves as the apex of the rocket with V-shaped streamers of color, shapes and values spewing outward to mark its course and create a feeling of movement.

Ken Paul

Here is a well-organized composition in watercolor by an excellent contemporary artist. The deer placed along the line separating the darker foreground from the lighter values of the middle distance makes a definite, yet unobtrusive center of interest. The natural flowing horizontal lines of the landscape are balanced and contained by the vertical thrust of the few defined evergreen trees. The color and busyness of the foreground, in contrast to the vagueness and close values of the background, create a convincing feeling of depth and space. In the same way the texture of the right corner is held in balance by the strong dark shape of the tree on the left.

Albin Henning

This plein air oil sketch done in Pomfret Center, Connecticut, shows that a focal area can be placed in the center of the composition without disastrous consequences. The white barn occupies almost the exact center of the canvas. In this case the bull's-eye placement works well enough because the surrounding areas are sufficiently diverse in color, value, and shape to overcome monotony. The variety in color, value, and texture between the foreground and the distant areas nicely establishes a feeling of depth and hilltop perspective.

Alfred Chadbourn

Ben Stahl

For this portrait, a popular contemporary painter has effectively employed the time-honored compositional plan based on a square within a rectangle. The principle works as well today as it did in the fourteenth century. It should be noted also that the subject's head is located exactly on the coordinates of the golden mean. Unquestionably, such placement was inadvertent. The artist, a longtime acquaintance and colleague, is known for his disdain for a calculated approach. With Chip's fine feeling for color and intuitive sense of design, formulas are an unnecessary encumbrance.

This delicious feast of color called The Star *is enhanced and made rich because of its subdued surroundings. It is an excellent example of a feeling of light produced through sacrifice, as discussed earlier. The single light source allows all the emphasis to be spotlighted, so the colors glow like a diamond necklace against dark velvet. Many pictures display a greater palette range, but most will fade in brilliance when compared with this gem. Notice the contrasts of edges, the varieties of shapes, the rhythms in the drapery, and the uplifted arms, along with the visual balance of the nicely placed details.*

Mark English

It is not likely many will find fault with this centered composition. Here an ace contemporary illustrator and painter demonstrates how delightful a forthright, in-the-middle placement can be. The variations offered in values, shapes, edges, and color are subtle, but extremely well considered. No monotony here. Everything is beautifully controlled, in both balance and harmony.

Andrew Wyeth

Painted while the artist was in his twenties, this watercolor is perhaps atypical of his more mature, meticulous renderings. It has, however, a certain refreshing dash and verve sometimes missing in his later work. Of note from the compositional viewpoint is the undisguised center placement. I hope by now the serious reader knows that such placement is not necessarily a design detriment. As the several examples prove, sometimes placing the focal area in the middle can be made to work just fine.

Fritz Henning

This painting illustrates the end of the era of the great steam trains. As the diagram at the right indicates, the composition is a pyramidal structure. The engine is the center of interest, with the key workmen given emphasis to explain the situation. Notice how the directional lines lead to the man with the cutting torch. The crane at the right repeats the triangular design and generates a secondary area of interest. The color is somber in keeping with the sadness we attach to the end of an epoch.

Fritz Henning

When the subject of the picture is a legendary 1870 Mississippi River steamboat race, you might conclude the concept and compositional approach to be self-evident. In general, it was. However, for historical accuracy a number of factors required special attention and research. Not only must the details of the vessels be correct, but the topography, the weather, and the conditions of the river demanded factual recording. Both vessels started at nearly the same time, and they actually raced against the clock. Only a few times in the three-day running between New Orleans and St. Louis did the rivals compete head to head. Obviously, such an occasion would serve best for an illustration.

As the sketches suggest, the original idea was to show a closer view of the foreboat. The cropping and crowding at the right made for drama, but it also reduced important identification features and gave the vessels something less than the required equal billing. In many ways this view would have made a more powerful picture.

The next thought was to move back as if the viewer were a spectator watching the scene from a more distant shore. The pattern of the smoke could be intriguing, but a feeling of speed was lacking. This led to a shifting of the boats toward the left, as shown in the final painting. Along the way I toyed with suggesting more action and conflict in the areas of the sky and water. Such compositional activity might generate more visual impact, but, alas, it also would have been counter to the facts. At such moments, it would be fun to have the abandon of Harvey Dunn and declare, "The author was in error." (See text on page 179.) For the illustrator, such action is seldom tolerable.

187

Aaron Shikler   *The New Britain Museum of American Art*

This beautifully composed and rendered portrait of the artist's wife was done in pastel on canvas. Again the composition utilizes the square—in this case, a rectangle—within a
rectangular format. The casual off-center pose is enhanced by
the repetitious vertical lines in the garment and the room's
structure. The straightforward simplicity of the picture's organization allows the observer to concentrate on the superbly
drawn details, value control and color. A splendid painting.

Bernard Fuchs

Besides a superb sense of color and technical facility, Bernie Fuchs has a gift of carrying his pictures to just the right degree of incompleteness. His finished work often retains the spontaneity and charm of a sketch. Unencumbered by unnecessary elaborations, he lets color, shapes, and value perform at their best.

Notice how simply every area is stated. The only touches you might call details—small highlights on the bridle and boots of the center horse and jockey—serve to acknowledge that this area is the focal center. No more refinements are necessary.

The concept for this type of picture stems from photographs. As the artist says: "Most of my pictures are based on informa-

tion recorded in my photographic shots. But, I don't shoot like a photographer . . . My photos are used only for reference and information. I am concerned with the mood or visual impact of a situation. . . . Usually many different photos are required, and I take all kinds of liberties in compressing or stretching them."*

However Bernie Fuchs does it, his sketch-like paintings with their marvelous rub-out effects, cast a touch of magic.

*North light, Vol 8, #6, 1976

The potency of color

The genesis of this painting was undoubtedly a photograph. As far as the shapes are concerned, it doesn't have much going for it. The repetitious rectangles of the building, background and roadway are monotonous. But the artist's use of strident colors along with finely controlled values do much to overcome the dullness of the shapes.

Briggs had a keen eye for the significant visual embellishment. He would study long and hard to uncover just the right detail or symbol and place it with care. Then he would purposely render it with the unconcerned freedom of an offhand sketch. Also of interest is the rhythmic movement of the boy at the right. It is an unusual action, yet here it seems just right. It is the kind of unique pose Briggs always looked for.

Austin Briggs

Milton Avery *Child's Supper*

The New Britain Museum of American Art
Gift of Roy R. Neuberger

Emil Nolde

Nolde painted numerous windmills of his native province in North Germany. Realistically recording the scene was not his purpose. Called an Expressionist, his works convey a dramatic, emotional response to his surroundings. Striking color and strong contrasts dominate most of his pictures.

Without the color this composition would be ordinary, not to say trite. Yet, the power of the color can not be denied. Because of it, the painting imparts a mood and essence of a place not often achieved through more faithful realistic renderings.

◄ Here the artist combines simplified shapes and poetic color to generate an appealing personal mode of expression. The harmonious organization of color stabilizes and makes effective what would otherwise be an indifferent composition.

Fritz Henning

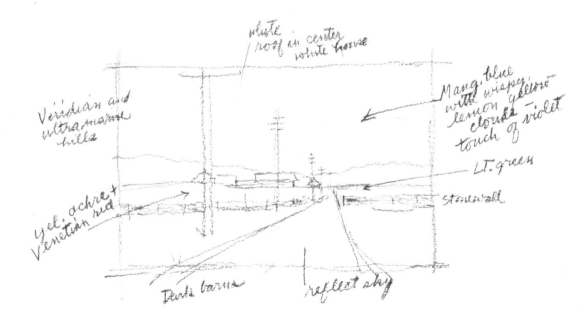

white roof in center
white house

Veridian and
ultramarine
hills

Mang. blue
with wispy
lemon yellow
clouds
touch of violet

LT. green

Yel. ochre +
Venetian red

stonewall

Dark barns

reflect sky

Slice of nature

Sooner or later every painter comes to learn the truth of the Whistler statement quoted in the margin. Seldom will the thoughtful artist discover the perfect slice of nature that only requires faithful recording. The view of the scene, its color, atmosphere, total environment, or small details may serve as the motivation for creating a picture; but hardly ever will it make a satisfactory composition without radical surgery. The color sketch on the opposite page is an example of the kinds of alterations necessary for a picture to fulfill its purpose—to express the artist's feelings and reaction to what he sees.

One chilly spring day, while driving near the small town of Sharon in the northwest corner of Connecticut, a scene down a side road attracted my attention. What intrigued me were the colors in the sky and the way the light played on a newly plowed field in the mid-distance. I stopped the car and made the thumbnail sketch and color notations shown below the painting.

The placement of the forms as observed are accurately described in the pencil rough. The road was straight and lined with telephone poles. The valley was fairly flat and the hills low in the distance. No painting was done on the spot. It was all fabricated later in my studio. The mediums were unorthodox—a combination of pastel and oil. They are compatible, and there is much to recommend their mixture.

As you can see, several alterations to the scene were made. First to be eliminated were the telephone poles. They were replaced with fence posts borrowed from the midsection near the stone wall. The straight road screamed for modification, as did the flatness of the valley floor. Flat and straight do not a proper New England make. The barns were left more or less intact but the farmhouse near them was moved back. A few tall verticals were needed to break the composition's dominant horizontal shapes, so pictorially an evergreen or two was planted along the wall. Finally, the hills were moved closer and given more altitude.   Any merit this sketch may have is not dependent on its accuracy in establishing the scene as it exists. Factual presentation is not the point. However, if you look at the picture, respond to the lighting and color, feel it was a chilly day but a rather pleasant place, and you wouldn't mind going a bit farther down that road—then we have communicated. When you think about it, that is not a bad accomplishment.

A final Whistler quote nicely wraps up these thoughts. He wrote: "That nature is always right, is an assertion, artistically, as untrue as it is one whose truth is universally taken for granted. Nature is very rarely right, to such an extent even, that it might almost be said that nature is usually wrong: That is to say, the condition of things that shall bring about the perfection of harmony worthy of a picture is rare and not common at all."

The imitator is a poor kind of creature. If the man who paints only the tree, or flower, or other surface he sees before him were an artist, the king of artists would be the photographer. It is for the artist to do something beyond this. . . .
James McNeill Whistler

Deceptive influences

Two pervasive conditions play havoc with everyone's judgment of art. One is subject matter. This is an individual reaction requiring constant introspection to avoid accepting or rejecting a picture based on artistic irrelevancies. That we love children, are fascinated by animals, boats, flowers, or are enthralled by mountain scenery should have but minimal bearing on our estimate of a painting. The second is a deceptive, sometimes subliminal factor, having to do with promotional influences generated for purposes only vaguely related to the artist's work. Such propaganda can be slick and disarming, or it can be spewed out with the unsubtle crassness of a carny con man. Both methods carry more weight than we would like to admit.

Since the burden of this book is to evaluate the whys and ways of worthy concepts and compositions, it seems fitting before signing off to examine pictures that have received acclaim and yet appear deficient in qualities purported to be vital. On this basis, let's discuss the paintings shown on pages 195 and 197. Both are by prestigious artists. Both have been extolled by critics. And both appear wanting in at least one key department.

Mary Cassatt was a fine painter, a legendary American who ranks with some of the best of her French Impressionist associates. As in this picture, she often painted and captured in color, attitude, and feeling the wondrous intimacy of mother and child. Unfortunately, in some instances she was so concerned with the figures and color she failed to give sufficient thought to the total design. True, many of her paintings can be classified as unfinished, at least as far as the background is concerned. Yet, because surrounding elements are included in some detail, the overall work must be faulted for placement.

In this case, notice the position of the pitcher in relation to the woman's head. Even in a preliminary sketch such juxtaposition is ill-advised. If we force ourselves to overlook the appeal of subject matter and judge the painting on the basis of shapes, values, color and design—the bedrock of all art—then, reluctantly, we must concede this composition has shortcomings.

Now let's take a careful look at Pablo Picasso and his painting called *Guernica*. This is a more complex and difficult situation to appraise, as both artist and picture are the subject of so much worldwide hype they are almost impossible to judge objectively.

"Picasso," wrote Frederic Taubes, "could never have reached [in the eyes of the public] a position matching that of Michelangelo without unprecedented promotion aided and abetted by the lack of standards in modern aesthetics."*

*Judgement of Art *by Frederic Taubes, published by North Light* ©1981.

Mary Cassatt

Whether or not you agree with this erudite art authority's assessment will probably depend on how much you have been taken in by the kind of publicity Taubes refers to. Many other tastemakers hold opposing opinions and parrot the notion that "*Guernica* is one of the strongest protests of all time against the horror of war."

Is the artist overrated? Is the painting worthy of veneration? If you could free yourself of all the influences you have heard or read about Picasso and this picture and evaluate it solely on its artistic merits, would you conclude it is a masterpiece?

The stark black, white, and gray painting, measuring about 12x26 feet, is impressive in scope and undeniably well designed. The solid pyramid structure is fragmented in an interesting variety of ways creating a tangled movement, rhythm, and balance between the interpenetrating planes. The dismembered, cartoon-like figures and animals establish several scattered interest areas, a drawback somewhat overcome because of the picture's size. As to the mood, what kind of feeling does it generate? Does its spirit move you to compassion and understanding? Does it speak to you directly, without outside embellishments, of the horror of being trapped in a city under bombardment?

To me it doesn't. Perhaps because I have been through bombings I find it difficult to relate to an intellectual approach to such an emotional experience. Depthless comic strip representations fail to symbolize for me the image of real people being killed, maimed, burned, and terrified.

If you did not know the work was a protest against the bombings by German aircraft of a Basque town during the Spanish Civil War, would you be able to differentiate between *Guernica*'s message and a number of other paintings by the artist done in a similar vein? Some of these pictures carry titles such as *Night Fishing at the Antilles, First Step,* and *The Muse.* It must be assumed these names bear some relationship to the subjects, yet the artist built these pictures with tortured, abused anatomy and fragmented shapes equally as brutal as those found in *Guernica.*

Why is Picasso's work in general, and *Guernica* in particular, enshrined in high esteem? The build-up has a long and interesting history. Not surprisingly, it consists of more than the usual gallery/agency hoopla, although that is substantial and noteworthy. More telling were the political circumstances of the day. Here are a few of the highlights.

Pablo Picasso was born and raised in Spain, but he spent most of his long career in France. He painted *Guernica* for the Paris International Exposition as a protest against the fascist forces of General Franco. The year was 1937 and the Spanish Civil War was in process. Franco was being supported by Hitler's Germany and Mussolini's Italy, while the Loyalist opposition was aided by Stalinist Russia. As a small-scale preview of World War II, the battlefields of Spain provided the antagonists a proving ground for their untested armaments.

Living in Paris, Picasso, a longtime Communist, was dedicated to the Loyalist cause and vowed neither he nor his paintings would return to his homeland until Spain was liberated. As a colorful character and a widely known avant-garde artist, many liberal anti-Fascist writers and newsmen found that the flamboyant expatriate made good copy. As a result, Picasso and *Guernica* were ballooned into symbols by an influential group of intellectuals who used the artist and his work to propagandize their popular anti-Fascist cause. The effect was a sustained public relations campaign that, because of the course of world events, continued for years.

Here is an example of the kind of "news" story that helped make Picasso a household word. It probably never happened, and assuredly it has nothing to do with the artist's painting capabilities.

Pablo Picasso   Yale University Art Gallery, New Haven
Fragmented shapes and abused anatomy are no strangers to many of Picasso's compositions. This one is entitled First Steps.

Pablo Picasso

Prado, Madrid

Hermann Goering, the notorious Nazi marshall of the German Luftwäffe, is said to have viewed *Guernica* in Paris when Picasso was present. Goering asked the artist, "You did this painting?" "No," Picasso is said to have replied, "You did."

Good story. Magnificent P.R. All the news services picked it up, and years later it is still making the rounds. Obviously, such publicity has no bearing on the merits of the picture, but it is naive to suppose it carries no influence. Galleries, of course, made the most of it; and the critics responded by *explaining* what might be viewed as inexplicable to the newly expanded audience. Clouded psychological analysis of the composition was interpreted, and hidden meanings were exposed—meanings, it is implied, normally only understood by the cognoscenti.

As paradoxical as it may seem, the most potent molders of taste in the art world are not artists. They are writers, the critics. For the most part, these power wielders secured their positions not because of their art scholarship or expertise, but because they can turn a provocative phrase. Hardly any have been involved in picture making. The publishers who hire

197

them feel this is proper, as it puts the writer on a level close to that of the viewing public. Initially the premise is sound, but the nature of the job soon isolates critics into a special cocoon. Like their counterparts covering the theatre and films, art reviewers are perforce exposed to such an array of showings and exhibits they quickly become jaundiced to any standard fare. In short order only the different and the unusual strike them as anything but dull or boring. On this basis, Picasso's work was a critic's delight.

But, you ask, what about the prominent artists and the others of the so-called Art Establishment—that unorganized group of museum directors, educators, connoisseurs, and artists, from whose ranks national committees and organizations such as National Endowment for the Arts are formed? Don't they have a voice? Can't they challenge promotional distortions, establish standards and allay public confusion? For many reasons this seldom happens. Consider these points.

● Artists rarely offer adverse public opinions of their contemporaries. To do so could appear self-serving and probably lead to unprofitable, unwanted public feuds. Also, they are deeply involved with their own work and most do not relish distracting interruptions.

● As guardians of the past, museum directors and curators of prestigious institutions who deal with the contemporary scene tend to be a cautious and myopic lot. However, they are loath to ignore art that is given critical acclaim and whose gallery prices appear on the rise. Historically, they know the value of much artwork appreciates with time. Like any competitive shopper, they don't want to pass up a bargain which in the future may be judged a priceless treasure. They are haunted by the shortsightedness of predecessors who failed to acquire, for next to nothing, once available works of unknowns such as Gauguin, Utrillo, and a host of others. Overreaction to the possibility of committing similar faux pas leads some to open the museum doors and checkbook to ballyhooed contemporaries of debatable quality. Whatever its merits, once a picture becomes a part of a collection those responsible for the acquisition will not readily admit to mistaken judgment. And once a major museum acquires a controversial contemporary work, others rush to follow suit. Any subsequent devaluation of the artist or the painting is considered a discredit to the directors and a loss for their institutions.

● The casual observer may not notice, but the sheltered world of academia is beset with insecurity, particularly at the administrative level. Heads of departments are more comfortable when the knowledgeable professor contents himself with teaching art appreciation with last year's lesson plans, rather than taking a public stand that might appear to be out of sync with the prevailing winds blown by the critics and supported by highly placed benefactors. Dwellers in the halls of ivy know the wisdom of the Oriental saying: "The nail that sticks out gets hammered in."

● As for the wealthy connoisseurs (if not rich, or potentially so, they are seldom considered), their interests are closely linked to those of the museums and the universities. Usually they are satisfied to stand aloof, keep an eye on their investments, look for bargains, and contemplate tax advantages.

This summary is oversimplified, but it suggests some of the motives the establishment has in maintaining conditions they helped manufacture. It is not a conspiracy to defraud or deceive, but it is obvious the vested interests of many influential parties come together, forging a formidable force for maintaining the status quo. A great deal of investment money and prestige depends on holding the line on commitments made to certain areas of "modern art."

As a consequence, a rational diagnosis of Picasso's work, as well as that of a host of others, remains mired in a maze of lofty sounding jargon fed to us by influential wordsmiths. In time things will surely change, but this will not come about soon. Aesthetic standards are difficult to establish in the heady atmosphere of high finance striding hand in hand with revolutionary vision. When the public is told they are being educated to a *new way of seeing,* who is to play the role of the innocent child in Hans Christian Andersen's tale and proclaim the emperor has no clothes?

Today, Vermeer and van Gogh, to name but two of many similar examples, are universally revered as great talents. During their lifetimes both were ignored as losers. The Dutch Master from Delft never sold a painting throughout his impoverished career; and the frenzied, romanticized van Gogh forever needed the financial aid of his brother. Conversely, a hundred years ago the darling of the art world was a Frenchman named Bouguereau. An excellent academic technician, he was, in his day, almost as successful as Picasso. But now his work is frowned upon and considered syrupy and secondrate.

A century from now how will Picasso and *Guernica* rate? Will they live on in their current near-sainthood status; or, will the power of promotion dim in the smog of time? Will Picasso, as Taubes suggests, be another Bouguereau, and his innovative vision be declassified to that of a frivolous footnote in art history; or, will he take a place alongside the Masters? Who knows? The jury will be out a long time. The balanced judgment of posterity should be available around the year 2050. Until then you will have to wait and weigh our own evaluations of the artist and his works against a torrent of deceptive influences.

William Adolphe Bouguereau
A century ago the sentimental works of Bouguereau made him rich and famous. Today his paintings are all but ignored.

199

Conclusion

To the faithful reader who has followed this far, I hope the examples shown and the thoughts expressed will re-enforce your approach in creating your own compositions and help in evaluating the works of others. Perhaps, along the way, you have gained a broader insight into different and useful ways of building pictures. As the varieties of illustrations demonstrate, styles and manners of expression can vary greatly. Each approach has advantages. Each has shortcomings. By whatever means, be it analytical or more intuitive, merit will find its way to your pictures when you follow procedures you prove to yourself are most useful.

Often the uninitiated are attracted to the skilled practitioner who performs with dazzling technique. This is logical. Showmanship and razzmatazz can be exciting. But they can also beguile you. The artist who becomes so enamored of rendering the surface, be it with finite finesse or bewildering boldness, usually is so intent upon his craft he forgets, or slurs over, the more important considerations of concept, structure, and meaning he hopes his painting will express. In short, he fails to reckon with everything we have spent so many pages discussing. Unfortunately, technique devoid of depth in planning and design usually fades quickly under knowledgeable examination. In the long run, technical skill without support functions in the picture about as effectively as a dance without rhythm, or a ladder without rungs.

One closing thought to consider.

Speed of accomplishment always plays a big role in our scheme of things. Students universally marvel at how fast an artist does a painting demonstration in a class or workshop. "Isn't it amazing," you hear, "how quickly he did it . . . such technique . . . so clever . . . why, it only took him forty minutes to complete the whole thing."

To be awed by speed is to misunderstand what picture making is all about. The virtuoso who whips off a pro forma painting in a few minutes undoubtedly spent hours in preparing and establishing his picture concept. He also put in years learning the legerdemain of his craft. In truth, speed and agility in performance have no bearing on the ultimate worth of a work of art. And ultimate worth is what it is all about.

List of contributing artists with capsule biographies.

Fra Angelico (Italian, 1387-1455) A Dominican monk, this Florentine painter sought to maintain art traditions in the service of the church. His frescos are noted for their economy in handling and enamel-like colors

Milton Avery (American, 1885-1965) Born in Altmar, New York, Avery studied briefly at Connecticut League of Artists. Although a recent biographer claims he had a more extended art education, the artist is considered to be self-taught through personal study of Fauvists and Expressionists. Many contemporary painters acknowledge a debt to his simple, poetic use of shapes and color.

George Bellows (American, 1882-1925) A pupil of Robert Henri and noted member of the Ash-Can School. He delighted in prize fight scenes and teeming city life.

Rosa Bonheur (French, 1822-1899) A highly successful animal artist, Rosa was trained by her father, Raymond Bonheur. Following her death, her romanticized work lost much of its popularity.

Pierre Bonnard (French, 1867-1947) Bonnard studied at Académe Julien in Paris where he was much influenced by the works of Gauguin. Later at École des Beaux-Arts he came to know Vuillard and Ronssel. He was also associated with the Fauves. Some regard Bonnard as the most important "pure painter" of his time.

William Adolphe Bouguereau (French, 1825-1905) An academic painter of sentimental subjects in a photographic style that earned him immense popularity during his day. His work is all but scorned today.

Austin Briggs (American, 1909-1973) Born in Minnesota, Briggs attended Wicker Art School, Detroit City College and the Art Students League in New York. A prolific and versatile illustrator who is respected for his innovativeness.

Pieter Bruegel (Flemish, c.1525-1569) Known as the Elder (he had two artist sons of lesser note), this Flemish Master followed in the legacy of Bosch. Outstanding are his lively and humorously detailed representations of village scenes of his day.

Mary Cassatt (American, 1845-1926) An expatriate who spent most of her life in Paris, Cassatt was a minor figure in the Impressionist movement. A friend of Degas and other notables of the day, she is admired for her splendid interpretations of mothers and children.

Alfred Chadbourn (American) Chadbourn studied at the Chouinard Art Institute in Los Angeles, at École des Beaux-Arts and the Académie de la Grand Chaumiere in Paris. A devoted landscape and still life painter, he has an accomplished approach and a fine feeling for color.

Paul Cézanne (French 1839-1906) A banker's son born at Aix-en-Provence, Cézanne studied at Académie Suisse in Paris and became friendly with many Impressionists. However, he pursued his own course of intellectual realism. Classified as a Post-Impressionist, he is thought by many to be the father of "modern art."

Marc Chagall (Russian, 1889-1981) Chagall studied in St. Petersburg and Bakst and came to École de Paris in 1910. Linked with the avant-garde, he is considered a French Expressionist and is acclaimed for his imaginative childlike approach.

John Constable (English, 1776-1837) Along with Turner, Constable is ranked as the foremost English landscape painter. He studied in London and was aided by Benjamin West. Many of Constable's quick on-the-spot sketches are more important than his finished compositions.

Gustave Courbet (French, 1819-1877) Courbet studied painting mainly on his own in Paris. Classified a radical figure, he led the movement away from the staid academic approach of the Salon toward a more natural spontaneity and a feeling of sunlight.

Jean Baptiste Corot (French, 1796-1875) Abandoning a business career at age 26, Corot became a pupil of a landscape painter named Michallon. Considered a Romantic, Corot idealized his realistic interpretations of country scenes.

Claude Croney (American) A native of Massachusetts known for his moody watercolors of New England. Most of his post-high school training was self-taught. A clever technician with a popular workshop following.

John Steuart Curry (American, 1897-1946) Born in Dunavant, Kansas, Curry studied at Kansas City Art Institute and the Art Institute of Chicago. A successful illustrator, but he is primarily remembered for his paintings of the Midwest.

Honoré Daumier (French 1810-1899) During his life Daumier was known mainly for the social satire of his popular lithographs of the Paris scene. In recent times the quality of his paintings has gained widespread recognition. In his later years he was nearly blind and subsisted on a small pension from the government.

Edgar Degas (French, 1834-1917) Trained as a lawyer, Degas entered École des Beaux-Arts in his 20's, and became acquainted with the Impressionists. He steered a solitary course and is not usually identified with any group. His sensitive eye, use of color, movement and compositional arrangement have gained him lasting recognition.

Harvey Dunn (American, 1884-1952) Born in South Dakota, Dunn studied at the Art Institute of Chicago and with Howard Pyle. An excellent painter, he was also an outstanding teacher. He adopted Pyle's teaching philosophy and had a great influence on several generations of illustrators. Some of his students include: Dean Cornwell, Harold Von Schmidt, Mead Shaeffer and Albin Henning. Dunn was a war correspondent in World War I.

Albrecht Dürer (German, 1471-1528) This giant of Western art lived most of his life in Nuremberg, but his accomplishments reached far beyond his medieval studio. His religious paintings and portraits rank with the best of his time, but his innovative talents truly excelled in graphic art. His woodcuts and silverprints set standards yet to be surpassed.

Thomas Eakins (American, 1844-1916) Eakins was born, raised and lived in Philadelphia. He had an uncompromising attitude for the factual and scientific visual statement. An inspired teacher, he had great influence on many younger artists of the day and for generations to follow.

Mark English (American) Born in Hubbard, Texas, English attended the University of Texas and the Art Center School in Los Angeles. A pacesetting artist whose sensitive renderings and controlled compositions have greatly influenced the style of illustration in the 1970's and 80's.

James Ensor (Belgian, 1860-1949) A native of Ostend and trained in Brussels, the artist is known for his macabre and bizarre subject matter.

van Eyck (Flemish, early 15th century) The brothers, Jan and Hubert van Eyck, are accredited with the founding of the Flemish School of painting. They are also considered to be among the first to use oil paint. Although their work is often indistinguishable, Jan in particular is noted for his technical skill and inventiveness.

Ignace Fantin-Latour (French, 1836-1904) Born in Grenoble and taught by his father, an Italian landscape painter. Fantin-Latour also studied at École des Beaux-Arts in Paris. A romantic who is best known for his sensitive figure groups and still lifes.

Jean Louis Forain (French, 1852-1931) An illustrator and caricaturist from Reims. Forain studied at École des Beaux-Arts. He was a friend of Cézanne and Lautrec. He is known for the expressive, satirical quality of his line.

Nicolai Fechin (Russian, 1881-1955) A native of Kazan where he studied and taught art. He came to the U.S. at age 42 and lived much of the time in the area of Taos, New Mexico. Outstanding are his charcoal drawings of Pueblo Indians.

Robert Fawcett (English, 1903-1967) Born in London and studied at the Slade School of London University. Fawcett spent most of his career in the U.S. where his reign as a top-flight illustrator spanned a period of more than 30 years. An outstanding draughtsman, he had superb control of pattern and intricate detail.

Bernard Fuchs (American) Born in O'Fallon, Illinois, Fuchs studied at Washington University in St. Louis. He began his career in Detroit doing car illustrations. He soon moved on to New York where his work has appeared in practically every major magazine. An outstanding illustrator with a fine sense of color and a feeling for the implied visual statement.

Vincent van Gogh (Dutch, 1853-1890) A colorful character whose artistic achievements are linked with the Post-Impressionists centered in Paris. A prolific painter, van Gogh's work is full of power and emotion. Disdained during his life, this mainly self-taught artist's work is now ranked among the giants of the art world.

Rube Goldberg (American, 1883-1970) Reuben Lucius Goldberg was trained as a mining engineer, but he spent his long career as a cartoonist. His name is in the dictionary to describe his deviously complex inventions that were a syndicated newspaper feature for years.

Francisco Goya (Spanish, 1746-1828) Born in Fuendetodos, Goya was the son of a master gilder. He worked mostly in Madrid where he became Court Painter. His portraits were noteworthy, but his inspired work were paintings and etchings dealing with the Spanish resistance to the forces of Napoleon.

El Greco (Spanish, 1541-1614) El Greco was born in Crete. His real name was Theotokopoulos. He spent most of his life in Toledo where he became famous as *The Greek*. Before going to Spain he studied in Crete and in Venice. El Greco is noted for his cool palette and his mannered distortions.

Frans Hals (Dutch, 1581-1666) Born in Antwerp, Hals lived most of his life in Haarlem. Primarily a portraitist, he was a virtuoso paint manipulator. He is said to have been beset with financial difficulties throughout his life. He is generally rated just below Rembrandt among the Dutch Masters.

Peter Helck (American) Born in New York City, Helck studied at the Art Students League and privately with several outstanding artists, including the British muralist, Frank Brangwyn. A dedicated artist of great capability, Helck is noted for his illustrations of historic auto races, trains and industrial subjects.

Albin Henning (American, 1886-1943) born in Oberdorla, Germany, he immigrated with his parents to St. Paul, Minnesota, in 1889. He studied at the Chicago Art Institute and with Harvey Dunn. He is known for his *Saturday Evening Post* illustrations of World War I and adventure stories for *American Boy* and other publications.

Robert Henri (American, 1865-1929) Painter and gifted teacher who studied and taught in Philadelphia and New York. A member of *The Eight,* whose revolt against academic restrictions fostered a realism movement that became known as the Ashcan School.

Joseph Hirsch (American, 1910-1981) Born in Philadelphia and studied at the Philadelphia Academy of Art. He also studied with George Luks. Hirsch taught at a number of schools including Chicago Art Institute, Art Students League, National Academy of Design, Dartmouth College and others. An excellent realistic painter, he is noted for his interpretation of the figure.

Winslow Homer (American, 1836-1910) A mainly self-taught naturalistic landscape, seascape and genre painter, Homer began his career as an illustrator. An innovator, he explored color and light through luminosity rather than the blurred approach of the Impressionists.

Edward Hopper (American, 1882-1967) A student of Henri, Hopper sold his first painting at the famous Armory Show in 1913. He soon advanced from the Ashcan School and developed a personal style. He is acclaimed for his formal presentations of stark, lonely street and city scenes.

Lynn Bogue Hunt (American, 1878-1960) Born in Honeoye, New York, his interest in wildlife led him to the study of taxidermy, where he thoroughly learned the anatomy of birds and animals. A knowledgeable animal illustrator, Hunt worked for many outdoor magazines.

Meindert Hobbema (Dutch, 1638-1709) A native of Amsterdam he studied with Jacob van Ruisdael. Generally, Hobbema painted a narrow range of landscapes. At age 30 he became a municipal clerk in Amsterdam, and practically gave up art.

Wassily Kandinsky (Russian, 1886-1944) born in Moscow where he studied law and political science. Abandoning a business career, Kandinsky moved to Munich at about age 30 to study painting. He spent much of his later life in France. Kandinsky is considered a founder of Abstract-Expressionism.

Oskar Kokoschka (German, 1886-1980) Of Czech and Austrian parentage, the artist lived and studied a number of years in Vienna. He was an early associate of Gustav Klimt. Kokoschka is known for his Expressionist landscapes and his so-called psychological portraits.

Paul Landry (American) Landry grew up in Halifax and went to the Nova Scotia College of Art, the Art Students League in New York and Rockford College, Illinois. He has earned recognition as a landscape and seascape painter in New England.

Leonardo da Vinci (Italian, 1452-1519) Probably the most variously accomplished artist of the Italian Renaissance. He is renowned as a painter, sculptor, architect, inventor and thinker. Few of his paintings have survived, but some, such as the Last Supper and Mona Lisa, are acclaimed as among the best in Western art.

Fred Ludekens (American, 1900-1982) A native Californian, Ludekens studied art briefly as a night student at University of California Extension. Successful in the dual roles of advertising art director and illustrator, he was outstanding at creating bold, visual page impact.

George Luks (American, 1857-1933) Luks studied with Henri and was one of *The Eight* who started the Ashcan School. Bohemian and unconventional in attitude, his work is somewhat uneven in quality.

Edouard Manet (French, 1832-1883) Manet studied in the studio of Parisian artist, Couture, but his painting style was influenced by study of the Old Masters, primarily Velazquez. He became linked with Impressionists, including Renoir and Sisley. Manet is noted for his high-key paintings in sunlight.

Tommaso Masaccio (Italian, 1401-1428) Born near Florence, Masaccio spent the final six years of his life in Rome. He died at age 27. In his short life he produced four major works. He has been referred to as the inheritor of Giotto and the artistic ancestor of Michelangelo.

John McDermott (American, 1919-1977) Born in Montana, McDermott spent most of his boyhood in California. Following high school he began working at the Disney Studios. After serving as a Marine combat artist in World War II, he became an illustrator in New York. McDermott made a number of 16mm movies of historic battles, some of which were shown on national television. He also authored several novels about artists under a pen name.

Michelangelo (Italian, 1475-1564) Among the greatest figures of the Renaissance, Michelangelo's sculptures are unequaled in power and quality. An extraordinary draughtsman, his frescos adorning the ceiling of the Sistine Chapel rank at the pinnacle of Western art.

Piet Mondrian (Dutch, 1872-1944) Born in Amersfoort, Mondrian studied at the Amsterdam Academy. He became a leader of the geometric abstract style which has had a continuing influence on contempory design.

Claude Monet (French, 1840-1926) The artist started to paint landscapes as a youth in Le Havre. Later he studied at the Académie Suisse in Paris. While studying with Gleyre he met Renoir, Sisley and Bazille. A friend of Pissarro, Monet is considered to have mainly taught himself from his contemporaries. He was an Impressionist, and is celebrated for his treatment of light.

Emil Nolde (German, 1867-1956) An Expressionist who studied in Munich and Paris. He was a member of the Dresden Brücke, and traveled considerably in the Far East and the South Seas. Known for strident color and distorted mask-like heads, his best works were moody landscapes of North Germany.

Al Parker (American) Al Parker was born and raised in St. Louis where he attended Washington University. At a tender age he became a popular illustrator for many national magazines. He is admired for his brilliant concepts and innovativeness.

Robert Peak (American) Born in Colorado, Peak received his art education at the Art Center School in California. His skill and facility in producing trendy illustrations have earned him respect and a rewarding career.

Maxfield Parrish (American, 1870-1966) Born in Philadelphia, Parrish spent much of his early life in his father's studio in New England. He studied at Haverford College, the Pennsylvania Academy and with Howard Pyle at Drexel Institute. His illustrations and paintings are remembered for their meticulous rendering and glowing glazes of theatrical color.

Kenneth Paul (American, 1906-1983) Ken Paul studied at the Chicago Art Institute and the National Academy of Art in Chicago. Much of his career was as an art director for major New York advertising agencies. He also did some magazine illustration. In recent years he devoted himself to watercolor painting.

Pablo Picasso (Spanish, 1881-1973) The son of a drawing master of Malaga, Picasso is recognized as a dominant influence of new art forms during the first part of the 20th century. A major force in Cubism and abstraction, he is known for anatomical distortions and experimental sculpture. The bulk of his later work is of questionable quality.

Camille Pissarro (French, 1830-1903) Born in the West Indies, Pissaro studied in Paris at the École des Beaux-Arts. He was early influenced by Turner and Constable, and later became associated with Signac and Seurat. He flirted with Pointillism, but is classified as an Impressionist. He helped Gauguin and was a friend of Cézanne.

Nicolas Poussin (French, 1593-1665) Although he worked most of his life in Rome, Poussin is considered to be the founder of French Classical Painting. He is famous for his mythological themes which are beautifully rendered in pastoral and poetic moods.

Howard Pyle (American, 1853-1911) Born in Wilmington, Delaware, Pyle began his art studies at age 16 under the tutelage of Philadelphia artist Van der Weilen. He also studied at New York's Art Students League. An outstanding illustrator and successful author, perhaps his greatest contribution is that of a teacher. He taught at Drexel Institute, and later conducted his own classes, free of charge, for gifted students. Among his fledglings were Harvey Dunn, N.C. Wyeth, Frank Schoonover, and many others who became noted illustrators in their own right.

Raphael (Italian, 1483-1520) The son of an Urbino painter, Raphael (his proper name was Raffaello Sanzio) was much influenced by Perugino and later by Michelangelo and da Vinci. His religious paintings for the Vatican established him as one of the foremost artists of the High Renaissance. He died at age 37.

Rembrandt van Rijn (Dutch, 1606-1669) The great Master was born in Leiden, and briefly studied at Leiden University. He spent most of his active career in Amsterdam. An artist of remarkable power, his paintings and etchings set standards yet to be matched.

Joshua Reynolds (English, 1723-1792) Born in Devonshire where his father was a headmaster of a grammar school, Reynolds studied art in London under an artist named Hudson. Clever and gifted, Reynolds became prominent for his portraits in the *grand manner*. The first president of the Royal Academy, he did much to elevate the status of artists in Britain.

Norman Rockwell (American, 1894-1978) Born in New York City, Rockwell never completed high school. He studied at the National Academy of Design and at the Art Students League. By age 21 he sold his first cover to *The Saturday Evening Post*. Through his long career he sold hundreds more and gained a popular recognition unsurpassed in the U.S. by any other artist. He is remembered for his warm, gentle, skillfully painted situations of an idealized America.

Salvator Rosa (Italian, 1615-1673) Rosa was born and lived near Naples, but he spent much time working in Rome and in Florence. He is called a Romantic painter, and is credited with introducing wild, broadly painted landscapes.

Peter Paul Rubens (Flemish, 1577-1640) A native of Westphalia, Rubens is considered the outstanding painter of his time. He studied in Antwerp, and spent much time in Rome and Paris. A master draughtsman and a painter particularly noted for his renderings of well-endowed female nudes.

John Singer Sargent (American, 1856-1925) Sargent was born in Boston and educated in Europe. He studied painting in Florence and Paris, but he spent most of his life in England. A brilliant technician, Sargent is famous for his fashionable society portraits.

Georges Seurat (French, 1859-1891) The young artist studied at École des Beaux-Arts in Paris. In collaboration with Signac, Seurat is credited with being the founder of Neo-Impressionism. He is noted for his Pointillist technique that depended on separate dots of color being mixed optically to generate a high degree of luminosity.

Alfred Sisley (French, 1839-1899) Sisley was born near Paris and studied with Gleyre. As a student he met Renoir and Monet. Grouped with the Impressionists, Sisley's range was limited, as he seemed content to represent the moods of weather and atmosphere.

Ben Shahn (American, 1898-1969) Shahn was born in Lithuania and came to the U.S. as a child. He began his art career as a lithographer's apprentice. Later he attended New York University, City College of New York and the National Academy of Design. In the 30's he worked with Rivera on the frescos at Rockefeller Center in New York. He also worked on W.P.A. art projects. He is noted for his penetrating drawings and paintings with biting social comment.

Aaron Shikler (American) Born in Brooklyn, the artist attended the New York High School of Music and Art. He also studied at the Tyler School, the Barnes Foundation and with Hans Hoffman. He is best known for his portraits of prominent people.

Joaquin Sorolla (Spanish, 1863-1923) Born in Valencia, Sorolla was raised by an aunt, as both of his parents died of cholera when he was two. At fifteen he entered the Royal Academy of San Carlos; he also studied for brief periods in Rome and Paris. Considered one of Spain's foremost artists, he is famous for his interpretations of dazzling sunlight.

Ben Stahl (American) Stahl began his career as an apprentice in an art studio of his hometown, Chicago. He quickly became a successful illustrator on a national level and later a versatile painter. Of note is his religious work for a special edition of the Bible and his Stations of the Cross paintings, all of which were stolen from a museum in Sarasota, Florida.

Gerard Ter Borch (Dutch, 1617-1681) Ter Borch, the Younger, studied with his father also named Gerard, known as the Elder. A precocious artist, the Younger is acclaimed for his small portraits and scenes of elegant society.

Giovanni Battista Tiepolo (Italian, 1696-1770) Tiepolo was a master of fresco decorative painting that carried strong Baroque influences. Many feel his work revived and enhanced the glories of Veronese and Tintoretto.

Henri Toulouse-Lautrec (French, 1864-1901) The son of a nobleman, Lautrec became permanently deformed as a result of childhood falls. He studied with portrait painter Joseph Bonnat and at the school of Fernand Corman. In his early 20's, his family set him up in a studio at Montmartre where he became friends with many notable artists of the Paris scene. He is remembered for his drawings, paintings and lithographs of the frolicking activities in Paris cabarets and brothels.

Diego Velazquez (Spanish, 1599-1660) Born and raised in Seville, Velazquez was apprenticed to an Italian painter named Francisco Pacheco. A virtuoso of paint handling and value control, Velazquez is famous for his direct, compassionate and revealing portraits.

Floris Verster (Dutch, 1861-1927) A still life painter who is mainly known for his small paintings of common household objects.

Harold Von Schmidt (American, 1892-1982) Von Schmidt grew up in California, studied at the California College of Arts and Crafts, and later with Harvey Dunn. He is noted for his western and adventure story illustrations.

Frank Webb (American) A native of Pittsburgh, Webb studied at the Art Institute of Pittsburgh and with such notables as Edgar A. Whitney. The popular watercolorist switched to painting and teaching after a successful career in commercial art.

Jan Vermeer (Dutch, 1632-1675) Vermeer is acclaimed for his genre paintings of his native city of Delft. Little is known of the details of his life other than he suffered financial difficulties. There is no evidence he sold any of his masterful paintings during his forty-three years of life.

Andrew Wyeth (American) The son of illustrator N.C. Wyeth, Andrew's popularity is based on his sensitive and meticulously rendered egg temperas and his subdued watercolors.

Anders Zorn (Swedish, 1860-1920) Widely traveled, Zorn lived at times in London, Paris, Spain, Algiers and Turkey. At first he was noted for his watercolors, later for his Sargent-like handling of oil. Most esteemed today are his etchings.

Reference sources

These are published works referred to in creating this book. It does not purport to be a complete bibliography covering all sources researched by the author over the years.

The Art of Appreciation by Harold Osborne; Oxford University Press, London © 1970

The Art of Painting by Leonardo da Vinci; Philosophical Library, New York © 1957

The Art of Painting by Albert C. Barnes; Harcourt, Brace and Co., New York © 1928

Art Through the Ages by Helen Gardner; Harcourt Brace Jovanovich, Inc., New York © 1980

The Art of Whistler by Elizabeth and Joseph Pennell; Modern Library, New York © 1928

Bruegel by Robert L. Deleroy; Skira, Lausanne, Switzerland © 1959

Cézanne by René Huyghe; Harry N. Abrams Inc. New York © 1962

Croney on Watercolor text by Charles Movalli; North Light Publishers, Westport, Conn. © 1981

The Cult of Art by Jean Gimpel; Stein and Day Publishers, New York

Degas by Camille Mauclair; The Hyperion Press, New York © 1941

Design Drawing by William Kirby Locard; Van Nostrand Reinhold, New York © 1982

Education of Vision by George Kepes; George Braziller, New York © 1965

Emil Nolde by Werner Haftmann; Harry N. Abrams, New York

Gertrude Stein on Picasso; Liveright Publishing, New York © 1970

22 Famous Artists by Mary Anne Guitar; David McKay Co., Inc., New York © 1964

How I Make a Picture by Al Parker; Institute of Commercial Art, Westport, Conn. © 1949

How I Make a Picture by Austin Briggs; Institute of Commercial Art, Westport, Conn. © 1952

How I Make a Picture by Robert Fawcett; Institute of Commercial Art, Westport, Conn. © 1949

How I Make a Picture by Norman Rockwell; Institute of Commercial Art, Westport, Conn. © 1949

Keys to Art by John Canaday; Tudor Publishing Co., New York © 1962

Letters of Great Artists, compiled by Richard Freedenthal; Random House, New York © 1963

Man and His Images by George Oeri; Viking Press, New York © 1968

Modern Art—19th and 20th Centuries by Meyer Schapiro; George Braziller, Inc. New York © 1978

Modern Painting by Maurice Raynal; Skira, Geneva, Switzerland © 1953

Monet by Denis Rouart; Skira, Lausanne, Switzerland

On Drawing and Painting by Paul Landry; North Light Publishers, Westport, Conn. © 1977

Oskar Kokoschka by Bernhard Bultmann; Harry N. Abrams, New York

Painting by Peter Owens; Oxford University Press, London © 1970

Pictorial Composition by H.R. Poore; G.P. Putnam's Sons, New York © 1903

Pioneers of Modern Art by W. Sandberg and H.C.L. Jaffé; McGraw-Hill Co., New York © 1961

Pioneers of Modern Art—The Stedelijk Museum, Amsterdam, The Netherlands

Pissarro by John Rewald; Harry N. Abrams, New York

Perception and Pictorial Representation edited by C.F. Nodine and D.F. Fisher; Praeger Publishing, New York

Renaissance edited by Richard M. Ketchum; American Heritage Publishing, Inc., New York © 1961

The Visual Arts as Human Experience by Donald L. Weismann; Prentice-Hall, Inc., Englewood, N.J.

The Visual Dialogue by Nathan Knobler; Holt, Rinehart and Winston, Inc., New York

Where Your Heart Is (Harvey Dunn) by Robert F. Karolevits, North Plains Press, Aberdeen, S.D. © 1970

World History of Art by Sheldon Cheney; Viking Press, New York © 1967

The World of Impressionists by Hans L.C. Jaffé; Hammond, Inc., Maplewood, N.J. © 1969

The World of Velazquez by Dale Brown; Time-Life Books, New York © 1969

INDEX